Cambridge Elements ☰

Elements in the Philosophy of Mind
edited by
Keith Frankish
The University of Sheffield

AFFECTIVE BODILY AWARENESS

Frédérique de Vignemont
*Institut Jean Nicod CNRS – EHESS – ENS – PSL
University*

CAMBRIDGE
UNIVERSITY PRESS

Shaftesbury Road, Cambridge CB2 8EA, United Kingdom

One Liberty Plaza, 20th Floor, New York, NY 10006, USA

477 Williamstown Road, Port Melbourne, VIC 3207, Australia

314–321, 3rd Floor, Plot 3, Splendor Forum, Jasola District Centre,
New Delhi – 110025, India

103 Penang Road, #05–06/07, Visioncrest Commercial, Singapore 238467

Cambridge University Press is part of Cambridge University Press & Assessment,
a department of the University of Cambridge.

We share the University's mission to contribute to society through the pursuit of
education, learning and research at the highest international levels of excellence.

www.cambridge.org
Information on this title: www.cambridge.org/9781009454100

DOI: 10.1017/9781009209717

When citing this work, please include a reference to the DOI 10.1017/9781009209717

First published 2023

A catalogue record for this publication is available from the British Library

ISBN 978-1-009-45410-0 Hardback
ISBN 978-1-009-20968-7 Paperback
ISSN 2633-9080 (online)
ISSN 2633-9072 (print)

Affective Bodily Awareness

Elements in the Philosophy of Mind

DOI: 10.1017/9781009209717
First published online: August 2023

Frédérique de Vignemont
Institut Jean Nicod CNRS – EHESS – ENS – PSL University

Author for correspondence: Frédérique de Vignemont, frederique.de.vigne mont@ens.fr

Abstract: Most accounts of bodily self-awareness focus on its sensory and agentive dimensions, tracking the origins of our special relationship with our own body in the way we gain information about it and in the way we act with it. However, they often neglect a fundamental dimension of our subjective bodily life, namely its affective dimension. The body typically remains at the margin of consciousness unless bodily information alerts us to the goodness or badness of our bodily states. This Element will discuss bodily self-awareness through the filter of its affective significance. It is organized around four core themes: (i) the relationship between bodily awareness and action in instrumental and protective contexts, (ii) the motivational role of pain and interoception, (iii) the sense of bodily ownership and its relation to the value of the body for survival, and (iv) bodily anchoring in peripersonal and egocentric awareness. This title is also available as Open Access on Cambridge Core.

Keywords: self, action, pain, interoception, egocentric

ISBNs: 9781009454100 (HB), 9781009209687 (PB), 9781009209717 (OC)
ISSNs: 2633-9080 (online), 2633-9072 (print)

Contents

Introduction

Though Descartes is known for his dualism, asserting that the mind and the body are of two distinct substances, one should not forget that he also highlighted the unique quality of the union between the two: 'Nature likewise teaches me by these sensations of pain, hunger, thirst, etc., that I am not only lodged in my body as a pilot in a vessel but that I am besides so intimately conjoined, and as it were intermixed with it, that my mind and body compose a certain unity' (Descartes, 1641/1979, Meditation VI). At the time, the Princess Elisabeth of Bohemia (1643) found his writings relatively elusive, and she wrote to him asking for further details about the relation between the mind and the body. Descartes replied: 'What belongs to the soul's union with the body is a very dark affair when it comes from the intellect (whether alone or aided by the imagination), but it is very bright when the senses have a hand in it' (Descartes 1643/2018: letter 28.v.1643).

The objective of this Element is to shed some light on this 'very dark affair', focussing on the unique way we experience our body.[1] Though the body is a material entity located in space and time in the same way as a rock, a tree, or a bird, we are aware of it in a distinctive manner that is not easily grasped. The question of bodily self-awareness, first exclusively addressed in the phenomenological tradition (Gurwitsch, 1985; Husserl, 1952/1989; Merleau-Ponty, 1945), has seen a recent boom in interest, especially over the last thirty years, both in philosophy and in cognitive science. It has been found to be a rich territory for philosophical explorations that provides a new angle in addressing general issues on perception, action, space, and the self.

Throughout the sections of this Element, I shall take as a guide the following apparently simple question: *what makes the awareness of our body unlike the one that a pilot has for a ship?* Most accounts of bodily self-awareness have focussed on its sensory and agentive dimensions, tracking the origins of the special relationship that we have with our own body in the way we gain information about it and in the way we act with it (e.g. Bermúdez, 1998; O'Shaughnessy, 1980; Shoemaker, 1976). We indeed receive a considerable quantity of signals sent by our body, not only through the classic five senses but also via a range of sensory receptors, what we may call *body senses*:

- Touch carries information about the external world (object shape, texture, and temperature) and about the body (pressure on a given region of the skin).
- Proprioception provides information about the position and movement of the segments of the body.

---

[1] See Chamberlain (2022) for a detailed treatment of Descartes's conception of bodily awareness.

- Nociception provides information about dangerously intense mechanical, mechanothermal, thermal, and chemical stimuli.
- Interoception provides information about the physiological condition of the body in order to maintain optimal homeostasis.
- The vestibular system provides information about body balance.

These systems, which are not under voluntary control, constantly carry a vast amount of information. Consider proprioception. It is based on receptors located on 400 joints, 570 muscles, and around 4,000 tendons. Interoception records around 20,000 breaths a day but also every single heartbeat, gastric pulsation, and so forth. As for the better-known sensory modality of touch, it relies on mechanoreceptors all over the 2 square metres of the skin surface, with the hand on its own having 17,000 receptors. Hence, the body is the object for which we receive the largest quantity of information, though mostly unconsciously to avoid the risk of cognitive overload. The difference with our awareness of other objects, however, is not only quantitative. We also have a special way of gaining information about our body. Through body senses, we can feel it *from the inside*. We feel the warmth of a cup of tea, we feel our legs crossed and our muscles tensed, we feel the softness of our bed, and we feel pain. The internal mode of our sensations has been conceived as the distinctive mark of bodily awareness. It has also been conceived as the signature of bodily agency (O'Shaughnessy, 1980): the way we control our body radically departs from the way a pilot controls his/her ship because of the internal access that we have to it. One might reply that a pilot can also *feel* the motion of the boat with eyes closed but his/her inner awareness of the ship is only indirect, mediated by bodily awareness. Direct inner access is restricted to one's own body.

Have we provided here an exhaustive list of the peculiarities of bodily awareness? One may note that the description remains so far relatively cold, so to speak. It neglects a fundamental fact about our subjective bodily life, namely that the body we consciously experience is too often the body that feels uncomfortable or even painful. Descartes (1641/1979) himself claimed that it is the 'sensations of pain, hunger, thirst, etc.' that teach us the unique relation between the body and the self. Those are bodily experiences that are affectively loaded and that invite us to take care of our body. In brief, we are not like pilots of a ship because a pilot can survive without a ship whereas our body seems to us irreplaceable and everything that happens to it directly matters to us.

Most research on agency has restricted its investigation to *instrumental agency*, focussing on positive interactions with the environment, from turning on a light to grasping a mug or kicking a ball. Instrumental agency allows us to act on the world, to explore it, and to manipulate objects. From an evolutionary point of view, its primary function is to find food and eat it. However, one should not neglect another class of movements, whose function concerns a different dimension of survival, namely self-defence. One can propose that it involves a distinct kind of bodily agency, which I call *protective agency*. Protective agency is sometimes summarized with the famous three Fs: freeze, fight, or flight. However, it is not restricted to innate reactions but also encompasses more sophisticated behaviours, such as grabbing an object to hide behind or washing one's hands. Nor is it limited to encounters with predators. At any moment, we avoid obstacles on our path, we retrieve our hand from the burning pot, we pay attention to our fingers when slicing carrots, we withdraw our foot when we see the heavy handbook ready to fall on it, and so forth. At first sight, instrumental and protective agency seem to utilize the same abilities, but when looking more closely, these two types of behaviours may not be exactly alike (Lang and Bradley, 2013). Compare the following situations. You are walking towards the dog to play with it or you are slowly walking away from it so that it does not jump at your throat. Arguably, the initiation of the protective movement is less under your voluntary control than for the instrumental one. Furthermore, your defensive response takes precedence over other plans, whereas playing is rarely at the top of your priorities. Finally, it is your concern for your body that motivates you to walk away, whereas consideration for your body seems to barely contribute to your intention to pet the dog.

Discussions on the complex relation between bodily agency and bodily awareness generally focus on proprioception, which informs us about the posture of our limbs in motion (e.g. Wong, 2015). However, if we focus on protective agency, we have to consider another major role played by bodily awareness, namely a motivational role. The body often remains at the margin of consciousness, but this is not true in protective contexts. Pain, interoception, and other affectively loaded bodily experiences, or even the mere anticipation of them, invite the subject to act, and their invitation has a unique motivational force. The challenge is to understand the contribution of affectively loaded bodily experiences for actions. It is also to understand what impact they have both for self-awareness and for the awareness of the world that surrounds the subject. Here, I shall propose that the special significance of the body for the subject's persistence is at the origin of the awareness that it is ours and nobody else's. I shall also argue that it gives a special salience to the environment and in particular to the immediate surroundings of the body, known as peripersonal space. This salience is not only behavioural. Objects are perceived in their spatial relation to the subject not only because he/she can act on them but also because they act on him/her and possibly hurt him/her.

This Element will thus discuss bodily self-awareness through the filter of its affective significance. It is organized around four core themes: the relation between bodily awareness and action (Section 1), pain, interoception, and other affectively loaded bodily sensations (Section 2), the sense of bodily ownership (Section 3), and self-location (Section 4). Each theme raises a number of questions that have been extensively discussed in the literature. Here, we shall bring to the limelight their affective dimension, which is too often neglected, and assess its impact for our enquiry into the unique nature of bodily self-awareness. There are many other things to discuss about bodily awareness, but by approaching it from the affective angle, we can raise a number of key issues that have recently animated the philosophical community.

1 The Acting Body

Descartes (1641/1979) posited his famous 'I think' at the core of self-awareness but Merleau-Ponty (1945) proposed replacing it by 'I can', thus bringing what he called the lived body (the body as we experience it without deliberately paying attention to it) and its agentive abilities to the forefront. On his view, bodily awareness primarily consists in being aware of the body in action. At first sight, it might seem indeed that the pre-eminent biological function of bodily awareness is to enable organisms to move and navigate in their environment, but to what extent are bodily experiences actually inseparable from actions? In this section, we shall consider three contemporary sensorimotor approaches to bodily awareness. Some of these conceptions focus on the contribution of bodily awareness for guiding action, whereas others describe the contribution of action for shaping bodily awareness. They can be summarized as follows:

(i)   Embodied agency view: bodily awareness is necessary for bodily guidance (Brewer, 1995; O'Shaughnessy, 1980).

(ii) Enactive view: bodily awareness consists in procedural knowledge of sensorimotor laws (Noë, 2004; O'Regan, 2011).

(iii) Dispositional view: bodily awareness is constitutively tied to our dispositions to act (Briscoe, 2009; Evans, 1982; Mandrigin, 2021).

The intuitive link between perception and action has been called into question by empirical dissociations between the two, primarily in the visual domain (Milner and Goodale, 2008), but, as we shall soon see, similar dissociations can be found for bodily awareness. We will assess the implications of these findings and discuss them in light of the functional distinction between two types of bodily representations, known as body schema and body image. We will then try to understand why, despite this duality, one still normally experiences a sense of unity between the body that one perceives and the body with which one acts. Finally, we will discuss how protective agency involves a distinctive type of bodily representation.

1.1 The Body in Action

Bodily information is required by the motor system to guide and monitor actions. At the early stage, the formation of intentions involves knowledge of one's bodily capacities, what one is able or unable to do. Then, the motor system needs to take the current bodily state and posture as inputs to plan the correct movements in detail. Proprioception can then provide direct internal access to this information. By contrast, when one moves objects other than one's body, such as a cursor on a screen, one needs to rely on vision only and control over the cursor is indirect, mediated by control over one's finger on the touchpad. O'Shaughnessy (1980, 1995) thus argues that the distinctive signature of embodied agency is that it necessarily depends on bodily awareness, which immediately presents from the inside the body part to act with.[2] I shall call this view the *embodied agency view*.

In what manner is bodily awareness required for action? The proposal is that its spatial content guides bodily movements. To do so, bodily awareness is in a specific format, a format that is directly exploitable by the motor system. Accordingly, it has been argued that the spatial organization of bodily awareness is based on some form of practical knowledge of the body (Anscombe, 1962; Brewer, 1995; McDowell, 2011; O'Shaughnessy, 1995; Wong, 2009): 'The intrinsic spatial content of normal bodily awareness is given directly in terms of practical knowledge how to act in connection with the bodily locations involved' (Brewer, 1995, p. 302).

On this view, bodily awareness presents to the subject what has been called *bodily affordances*, which consist in 'what possibilities of movement are open to one' (Wong, 2009, p. 45). It is thanks to the practical knowledge of bodily affordances that one does not attempt to move in biologically impossible or painful ways. It is also thanks to it that one does not over- or under-reach when trying to grab an object. This knowledge is built on the basis of motor expertise gained thanks to repeated past sensorimotor feedback:

> Then in an analogous practical sense we all of us have knowledge of our limb spatial possibilities; so that a man will introduce his hand into a cupboard but will not attempt to insert it into a thimble! Indeed through assembling the

---

[2] To be clear, the claim is not that bodily awareness is sufficient. Arguably, most part of fine-grained control can be based on unconscious sensorimotor transformations.

lowest common denominator of all the acts he will undertake with his hand, we might finally manage to assemble a sort of 'practical photograph' of the hand. (O'Shaughnessy, 1980, p. 225)

The hypothesis is thus that the spatial organization of bodily awareness follows motor rules so that it can guide actions. The problem, however, is that different spatial principles are at work for perception and for action. Let us consider body mereology, which corresponds to the segmentation of the body into parts. In one study, participants were asked to judge distances between two tactile stimuli. It was found that the stimulations felt more separated if they were applied across the wrist on two distinct body parts (on the hand and on the forearm) than within a single body part (within the hand or within the forearm) (Vignemont et al., 2009). This result is consistent with the category boundary effect: discriminability is increased between categories and reduced within categories (Pastore, 1987).[3] The body that we perceive is thus structured into *well-segmented* categorical body parts individuated by joints (Bermúdez, 1998). By contrast, actions require *holistic* representations of groups of bodily effectors united by motor commands. When moving, the segments of the body that are involved are brought together to form functionally coherent synergies. Interestingly, when participants were asked to actively move their wrist several times before receiving the two tactile stimulations, it was found that they overestimated less the distance between them, thus showing a reduced tendency to segment the body into categorical parts (Vignemont et al., 2009). This finding illustrates that spatial representations of the body differ in active and passive contexts.

Another way to investigate the relationship between bodily awareness and action is to assess to what extent agency is fundamentally altered when bodily awareness is disrupted (Wong, 2015, 2018). The case of peripheral deafferentation (deficit of afferent proprioceptive and tactile inputs) is of special interest here. In particular, two patients have been extensively studied, GL and IW. They lost proprioception and touch for their whole body below the neck after a disease that attacked their peripheral nervous system. As a consequence, with their eyes closed, they did not know the location of their limbs and they even reported feeling as though they were 'nothing but a head'. The first few months after their disease, they were bedridden because they had no control over their limbs, though their motor nerves were spared. So far, this is consistent with the embodied agency view but this incapacity to act did not last long. With time, these patients learnt to exploit visual information to calibrate and guide

---

[3] For instance, two shades of colour seem more different if they belong to two distinct colour categories than if they do not.

their movements so that they could move almost normally. For a naïve observer at least, one could fail to notice anything unusual in their case. Hence, though they did not feel the location of their limbs from the inside, they still achieved perfect control with them. Interestingly, KS, another deafferented patient but who was born without proprioception and touch, also succeeds in controlling her body on the basis of vision only (Miall et al., 2021). Deafferentation thus falsifies O'Shaughnessy's view: action cannot require bodily awareness since deafferented patients manage to move successfully.

Nonetheless, it has been repeatedly argued that these patients' agency is not similar to normally embodied agency (Brewer, 1995; Gallagher, 2022; Gallagher and Cole, 1995; Wong, 2015, 2017). On this view, despite their regained ability to move, they control their body like an external object. Whereas most movements are normally performed automatically without the need for attention, these patients have to look at their limbs to check their location and visually guide them until they reach their goal. Deafferented agency is then described as being *more reflexive* and *more visual* than embodied agency. Brewer (1995, p. 302) concludes that, unlike us, deafferented patients are like sailors on a ship, doomed to exclusively use vision, which presents their body from the outside.

However, one should not assume that embodied agency is purely on what one may call a zombie mode, which is based on unconscious processes only. Conscious control can also causally contribute to embodied agency (Shepherd, 2015). Conversely, deafferented agency can also operate on zombie mode. It is true that when the disease first stroke the patients had to explicitly learn how to exploit visual information and to focus on what they were doing, but, years later, did moving still require the same effort from them? Like for any skill the learning phase is cognitively costly and reflexive, but with practice actions normally become automatized; and though one still needs to process a large amount of information, one does not need to think about what one is doing. It appears that, at least in some of the deafferented patients, action monitoring had become automatic. For instance, the congenitally deafferented patient KS is able to write and draw in the same way as control participants, even when she has to simultaneously perform an audio-verbal echoing task that adds cognitive demand (Miall et al., 2021).[4]

In addition, deafferented patients are not the only ones to use vision. This sensory modality is the primary source of information about the world in which we act. It is also one of the main sources for our body, compensating for the intrinsic limitation of body senses. Proprioception has indeed limited reliability

---

[4] Patient GL also described to me that she felt on automatic mode (personal communication).

and precision. Its accuracy decreases with the number of joint angles that must be computed: the more distal the body part, the more complex the computations and the noisier the signals. In addition, after a few minutes of complete stillness, proprioceptive signals become weak. On the contrary, vision provides highly accurate information, which is more reliable than proprioception for vertical and horizontal directions in space. It is thus exploited by the motor system, even sometimes at the expanse of proprioception. In one study, healthy participants had to draw a line to reach a target and they received visual feedback only on the drawn line and not on their hand that was drawing it. In some trials, a spatial bias was artificially introduced so that the line they could see was deviated by a certain angle from their actual drawing. Yet they used the visual information to guide the rest of their movement (Fourneret and Jeannerod, 1998). Vision is thus pervasive in bodily control, no matter whether or not one is deafferented. In what sense, then, is deafferented agency different from embodied agency?

Finally, though they are rarely discussed, one should not forget the preserved bodily sensations that deafferented patients can still experience. They can still feel pain, thermoception, and affective touch, as well as thirst, hunger, and other interoceptive experiences (Olausson et al., 2008). Hence, they can still experience their body from the inside and their preserved bodily awareness can still intrinsically motivate their actions, even though it cannot guide them. For instance, they can go and get something to drink because they feel thirsty, or they can withdraw from the fire because they feel too hot. In brief, they are not like pilots on a ship. One cannot fully understand the complex relationship between bodily awareness and agency if one focusses exclusively on postural information. We need to know where each segment is located because the body is the primary effector of our actions, and also sometimes the target of our movements. However, one should not conceive of the role of bodily awareness only in terms of guidance. As I shall argue in Section 2, bodily awareness can also be the motivating reason for which we act. It is because we feel pain, hunger, or tiredness that we engage in specific behaviours, and one cannot explain what we do without referring to bodily awareness.

1.2 Action in the Body: The Enactive View

Our first question was in what manner bodily awareness contributes to action. We can now ask the reverse question: in what manner does action contribute to bodily awareness? Imagine that you are looking for your keys in your backpack. You put your hand in it and carefully explore its content with your fingers, item by item, until you find your keys. There is a sense in which your tactile awareness is gained through movements. In his book *Action in Perception*, Noë (2004, p. 1) makes the provocative claim 'All perception is touch-like'. By that, he means that perceptual experiences are inseparable from the perceiver's bodily activities. In his view, perception is not merely a means to action. Instead, perceptual experiences *constitutively depend* on the ability to keep track of the interdependence between sensory inputs and motor outputs (how sensory signals are modified by one's movements or by object motion). This view falls under the enactive approach to the mind, which argues that cognitive capacities constitutively depend on dynamic interactions between the body and its environment. The enactive approach is far broader than the sensorimotor account of perceptual experiences, but for sake of simplicity I shall refer to this specific claim as the *enactive view*. We shall now look at two distinct ways it can be applied to bodily awareness.

When you explore the content of your backpack, the way the objects feel in your hand changes depending on how you hold them. One may then talk of perspectival properties (how objects appear to the perceiver given a specific viewpoint). There is a sense in which you also experience the unique shape of the object that allows you to recognize it. One may then talk of objective properties (properties of the objects independently of their being perceived). The crucial question is how to go from the experience of perspectival properties to the experience of objective properties. According to Noë (2004), one has access to objective properties in virtue of one's procedural knowledge (or know-how) of the relation between the sensory incoming signals and bodily activities. For instance, you implicitly know how the tactile signals that you receive will change if you rotate the object in your hand. Notwithstanding whether this is the right account of haptic touch, we can ask whether we can generalize it to bodily awareness. One difficulty immediately arises. The distinction between perspectival and objective properties cannot be easily applied when it comes to the body that one experiences *from the inside*. Varying perspectives normally involves changing the spatial relation between the perceiver and the perceived object, but how could that work for bodily awareness? One can reduce the distance with an object, but one cannot get closer to one's body. One can look at it from different angles, but one cannot *feel it* from different angles. In brief, one cannot change the spatial conditions under which one's own body is felt from the inside.

One might then consider a different way to spell out the enactive view. O'Regan (2011), for instance, offers the following example: 'If you actively move the part of the body being touched, the incoming sensory stimulation will change ... What we mean by feeling something in a particular place in our bodies is precisely that certain sensorimotor laws apply' (pp. 157–8). Imagine that a spider lands on the back of your right hand. According to the enactive view, feeling its contact on your right hand consists in knowing that, if you move your left hand towards its location and remove the spider, it will stop the stimulation. But how do you know that it is this specific location (your right hand) that must be the target of your movement? In order to act upon (or with) a given body part, you need first to single it out and, for fear of circularity, this cannot be done on the basis of tactile-motor laws such as the ones described above. One can then posit another mechanism, possibly at the subpersonal level, that individuates the relevant location, but what role is left for sensorimotor contingencies to play if it is not to determine where one feels bodily sensations?

In addition to these conceptual difficulties (for further details, see Vignemont, 2011), one can also question the enactive view in light of empirical findings. Let us first consider the rubber hand illusion (RHI), originally discovered by Botvinick and Cohen (1998) and which has played a key role in recent discussions on bodily self-awareness. In the classic set-up, participants sit with their arm hidden behind a screen while fixating on a rubber hand presented in their bodily alignment; both the rubber hand and the real hand are then stroked simultaneously. After synchronous stroking, when asked to judge the location of their hand, participants mislocalize it in the direction of the location of the rubber hand. The enactive view might want to account for this in terms of erroneous sensorimotor laws: participants localize their hand closer to the location of the rubber hand because they are misleadingly induced to expect that, if they reach for this location, they will touch their own hand. However, it has been found that, at the sensorimotor level, participants can remain insensitive to the illusion: their movement is accurate when asked to reach for their hand (Kammers et al., 2009). Hence, the illusory spatial content of the bodily experience cannot be determined by the sensorimotor knowledge that correctly represents the position of the touched hand.

Other results are also difficult to account for by the enactive view. Consider the following description given by a patient amazed at her own ability to point to the site at which she was touched on her hand, though she felt absolutely no sensation of having been touched: 'But, I don't understand that. You put something there; I do not feel anything and yet I got there with my finger. How does that happen?' (Paillard et al., 1983, p. 550). This patient suffered from what is known as 'numbsense' (also called 'blind touch'). Following cortical or subcortical lesions, patients with numbsense feel completely anaesthetized on their right side: they are not able to detect, localize, or describe tactile stimuli. Nor are they able to indicate on a picture of an arm where the stimulus is applied, even in a forced-choice condition (Rossetti et al., 1995). Yet, despite their apparent numbness, they are able to guide their opposite hand towards the approximate site at which they are touched when so instructed and to their own surprise.[5] Likewise, although they are unaware of their arm location, they can accurately reach it. Hence, their sensorimotor knowledge is preserved but it does not suffice for the patients to have proprioceptive and tactile experiences. Even when they are simultaneously performing the movement to reach the location of the tactile stimulation, their tactile judgements do not improve. On the contrary, they perform poorly not only in the verbal task but also in the motor task (Rossetti et al., 1995).

Further dissociation between bodily experiences and sensorimotor knowledge can be found in the following study done on two brain-lesioned patients, KE and JO, who could still feel touch, unlike the patient with numbsense (Anema et al., 2009). They were asked to point to the location of tactile stimulations either on their own hand or on a hand drawing. Interestingly, it was found that JO succeeded for her own hand but not on the drawing, whereas KE pointed correctly to the drawing but not to his own hand. One way to interpret these results is that JO had intact sensorimotor knowledge but it did not suffice for providing her tactile experience with accurate spatial content. By contrast, KE's sensorimotor knowledge was impaired and yet he still had accurate tactile experiences: the former was thus not necessary for the latter.

To sum up, in both patients and healthy individuals, the spatial content of bodily awareness can be dissociated from the spatial information encoded in sensorimotor knowledge used to guide reaching and pointing movements so that they can be inaccurate in one and not in the other, and vice versa. Hence, sensorimotor knowledge, as recruited by instrumental movements, is neither necessary nor sufficient for bodily experiences.

How do the enactive advocates respond to these cases? O'Regan (2011) proposes that the spatial content of bodily experiences consists in a list of sensorimotor laws in multiple sensory modalities, including vision. For instance, if I turn my head towards the location that is touched, I will see what is touching me. Visual expectation can then explain the results found with the RHI and possibly other cases. One worry here is that, by making the list of sensorimotor laws multisensory, it might become almost impossible to falsify the theory. Noë (2010), on the other hand, claims that not all relations between perception and action are of interest to the enactive view but only those that are said to be non-instrumental (Hurley, 1998). In brief, what matter are actions that ground perceptual experiences, and not actions that are guided by them. Reaching or grasping movements, on his view, are mere 'practical consequences', and thus irrelevant for the enactive view. The challenge for Noë is

---

[5] Medina (2022) suggests that patients with numbsense have more conservative criteria for detection than for localization.

to determine which specific procedural knowledge is relevant. For haptic touch, he can highlight exploratory movements because they allow the perceiver to gain access to the objective properties of the touched objects. For bodily awareness, there seems to be no equivalent.

1.3 Action in the Body: The Dispositional View

We have just seen that Noë disqualifies from his account actions that are guided by perception, such as reaching. Yet those are the actions that are at the core of what is called the *dispositional view*, which is inspired by Gareth Evans's theory of egocentric experiences (Evans, 1982, 1985; see also Briscoe, 2008, 2014; Mandrigin, 2021). As we shall see in more detail in Section 4, Evans argues that the spatial content of perceptual experiences should be conceived as a 'behavioural space', defined as a complex network of links between percep-tion and dispositions to act: 'Having spatially significant perceptual information consists at least partly in being disposed to do various things' (Evans, 1982, p. 155). According to Evans, it is in virtue of being disposed to act on the world that perception has egocentric content, representing the location of the object in its spatial relation to the perceiver that may act on it. Unlike the enactive view, the dispositional view is thus based on the functional role played by perception for action (Briscoe, 2014). Evans focusses on visual, auditory, and haptic experiences, but he argues that all perceptual experiences share the same egocentric frame and thus the same behavioural space.[6] One can then offer a dispositional view of bodily experiences: 'So, experience of location in bodily awareness is constitutively tied to having dispositions to engage in bodily actions directed towards that bodily location' (Mandrigin, 2021, p. 1890). Mandrigin's objective is to explain the spatial structure of bodily experiences, which has been described by O'Shaughnessy (1980, p. 165) as 'feeling-in -a-certain-body-part-at-a-position-in-body-relative-physical-space'. In other words, we experience sensations not only in bodily or somatotopic coordinates (where in the body?) but also in egocentric coordinates (where is the body part relative to the rest of the body?). Let us return to the example of the spider landing on your right hand. On the dispositional view, your experience of the egocentric location of the contact is constitutively tied to your dispositions to move towards the location of your right hand. This does not entail that the spatiality of bodily awareness consists in sensorimotor knowledge. The claim is

---

[6] In reply to Molyneux's problem, he argues that a person born blind could immediately identify a shape previously familiar only by touch if he/she regained sight and was made to see it because vision and touch share the same egocentric content.

only that dispositions to act explain the fact that your tactile experience is felt to be located *in your right hand*. As a consequence, if there were a purely sentient statue that can perceive but not act, its bodily experiences would be spatially organized in a manner different from us, lacking egocentric frame of reference. It would feel only 'in-a-certain-body-part', but not 'at-a-position-in-body-relative-physical-space'.

The question then arises, do the dissociations that we described earlier in this section threaten the dispositional view? Here, I shall focus the discussion only on the RHI, but the same explanatory work could be done for the other findings. In the RHI, participants perceptually mislocalize their hand, showing that the egocentric content of their bodily experiences is inaccurate. However, they correctly guide their hand movements, showing that their behavioural space has not been influenced by the illusion. One may then conclude that the experience of location in bodily awareness is not constitutively tied to dispositions. However, Mandrigin (2021) rejects this conclusion. On her view, there is no dissociation between perception and action in the RHI; there is only a dissociation between different spatial frames of reference. More specifically, in the case of the RHI, she notes that participants are asked to localize their hand using visual cues. They thus need to remap proprioceptive signals into the visual reference frame, and this is where the illusion strikes. By contrast, she claims that participants do not need vision to guide their reaching movements towards their hand. They only need to remap proprioceptive signals into the motor reference frame. According to Mandrigin, the dissociation thus only shows that the erroneous remapping from proprioception to vision does not contaminate the remapping from proprioception to action.

However, one may doubt that this explanation suffices. Visual remapping is essential for the illusion to happen, but it is also required for motor responses. As discussed earlier in the case of deafferentation, vision is the sense of space par excellence and it influences – and sometimes even dominates – proprioception while acting. This is well illustrated by using prisms inducing visual distortions. With prisms, one sees one's hand at a location displaced towards the left or the right, depending on the type of distorting lens. There is then a visuo-proprioceptive conflict, but it is immediately solved in favour of vision: one instantly feels one's hand as if it were located near its displaced optical position. This phenomenon, known as visual capture, also affects bodily movements. In one study, participants saw their prismatic displaced hand on a table, and they were asked to point beneath the table to the *felt location* of their index finger with their contralateral hand. It was found that their pointing response was biased toward the *seen location*, although visual information was irrelevant to perform this task (Welch et al., 1979). In other words, the remapping from proprioception to action was contaminated by vision. This effect can be explained by the fact that all sensory inputs are remapped by default into an externally anchored supramodal reference frame, which can be directly used by the motor system (Pouget et al., 2002). Surprisingly maybe, this supramodal remapping occurs even when the task could be performed within a modality-specific reference frame. It predominantly exploits the eye-centred coordinate system, unless one is congenitally blind. This reflects the dominance of vision for manual control during ontogeny (Röder et al., 2007). If we return to the RHI, we can now see that the dissociation between the perceptual and the motor responses cannot be explained away in terms of distinct frames of reference. Even action involves remapping the location of the rubber hand into the eye-centred reference frame.

To conclude, the location in which we experience bodily events does not always coincide with the location towards which we are disposed to act. This is problematic for the dispositional view, but these dissociations were to be expected. Indeed, the rules that govern action are not the same as those that govern bodily awareness. They require different transformations of sensory signals, different spatial organizations, and make different cognitive demands. It has thus been suggested that we have at least two distinct kinds of bodily representations, the body schema and the body image (Ataria et al., 2021; Dijkerman and de Haan, 2007; Gallagher and Cole, 1995; Paillard, 1999; Vignemont, 2010). There are many disputes on the exact definition of these notions, and I shall not cover all their interpretations here. I shall only focus on their functional characterization.

1.4 Body Schema and Body Image

In order to best understand the difference between body schema and body image, one needs to understand their respective direction of fit (Anscombe, 1957). A mental content is said to have a 'mind-to-world direction of fit' when it describes a certain state of affairs and it is true when it matches it. Typically, visual experiences have a mind-to-world direction of fit: when I see the sky as blue, my visual content is accurate if it matches the actual colour of the sky. By contrast, a mental content is said to have a 'world-to-mind direction of fit' when the world must be made to match the content of the representation for it to be successful. Typically, intentions have a world-to-mind direction of fit: my intention to grasp the mug is successful if I grasp the mug. Within this theoretical framework, one can then claim that the body schema has both directions of fit, while the body image has only a mind-to-world direction of fit.

More specifically, the body schema can be conceived as the representation that carries precise information about the body in a format directly exploitable by the motor system to guide action planning and control. It plays both a descriptive and a directive role. It describes more or less accurately bodily parameters for actions (mind-to-world). It also prescribes the kind of movements that the body can perform (world-to-mind). It is then said to be correct if the movements are accomplished successfully (Clark, 1997; Grush, 2004; Millikan, 1995). The body image, on the other hand, corresponds to the percept that we form of our body, which feeds bodily experiences. It is built on the basis of the body schema but enriched by other inputs. Its content is exclusively descriptive. It must fit with the state of the body to be accurate (mind-to-world).

Arguably, the body schema is evolutionarily prior. Sensory processing evolved, in the first place, not to provide conscious perceptual experiences but to provide bodily control. It was only later in evolution with the emergence of more complex behaviours that sensory processing evolved to provide internal models accessible to other cognitive systems. The body schema is also developmentally prior. Young infants first engage in repetitive actions on their own body and explore visual-proprioceptive correspondence. The primacy of the body schema can finally be explained by the fact that it has to be more fine-grained and more reliable than the body image, which tolerates a larger margin of errors. You must represent the size of your limbs correctly for your actions to be successful, but there are no major consequences in being mistaken in your perceptual judgements about your body. Roughly speaking, it does not matter if the perception of the body is false as long as actions remain unaffected. On the other hand, the body image gains in richness what it loses in accuracy. The body schema is functionally restricted: it encodes only information about the bodily properties required for planning and controlling action. The content of the body image may not be as precise, but it carries information about more properties. This is true of perception in general: perceptual content is richer, and thus, more informative, than sensorimotor content.

Despite these functional differences, the subject still normally has a sense of acting with the same body as is perceived. This can be explained by the fact that both types of bodily representations contribute to bodily awareness but also by the fact that they interact together. Even if action control is based on sensorimotor transformations, one can refer to what one perceives to explain why one acts in a certain way, why one does this rather than that to achieve one's goal. Bodily experiences would not be able to provide valid justification of actions if the body image departed too much from the body schema. Though we have focussed so far only on cases in which action and bodily perception are dissociated, the fact is that cognitive systems generally tend to avoid inconsistency as much as possible. One can then propose that the two bodily representations can recalibrate each other to avoid too much discrepancy (Pitron et al., 2018).[7]

The notions of body schema and body image have been shown to be useful to explain a number of empirical results. Still, one should note that they both function as general terms that group together various bodily representations. One can then propose more fine-grained distinctions. The notion of body image has attracted most attention (and controversy) because of its heterogeneity, including not only perceptual aspects of the body but also affective and semantic dimensions (Gallagher, 2005). The body schema faces a similar problem of unity. Evans (1985) repeatedly claims that there is a unique behavioural space and most discussions on the relationship between bodily awareness and agency tend to assume a relatively univocal notion of action. However, as mentioned in Introduction, one must distinguish between instrumental and protective agency. I will now argue that these two forms of agency correspond to two distinct types of body schema: the working body schema and the protective body schema.

1.5 Working Schema and Protective Schema

The main measures of the body schema in neuropsychology consist in asking patients to point or reach for one part of their body, to perform routine daily actions such as dressing up, and to imagine mentally rotating their hand (Schwoebel and Coslett, 2005). Surprisingly, however, patients are almost never asked to perform protective movements like avoidance and withdrawal. One may reply that they involve the same type of body schema and therefore do not deserve to be specifically tested. But is this really the case? Ideally, one would need to be able to compare the two types of movements within the same study. As far as I know, this has never been done. Nonetheless, some findings can be taken as evidence that instrumental and protective agency recruits two distinct types of body schema.

Let us consider tool use. Tools extend our agentive abilities, allowing us to act further away and in new ways. As a consequence, they can be integrated into our body schema, as shown by numerous results. In one study, after having repeatedly used a long mechanical grabber, participants perceived their arm to be longer and the kinematics of their movements was significantly

---

[7] It may be that it is only if the discrepancies are persistent across time that the representations are realigned. This might explain why dissociations are found often for bodily illusions, which are extremely brief, or just after strokes in patients, but not later.

modified, as if their arm were elongated. This was so even for movements that were never performed with the grabber (Cardinali et al., 2009). Even though tools do not look like body parts, they can be integrated into the body schema. Though it is called *body* schema, it represents not only bodily effectors but also some external objects that extend motor abilities.[8] This is true, however, only for instrumental movements. If we consider protective agency, it becomes less clear that tools are represented in the same way as body parts. We need to keep tools in good shape in order to be able to use them, but if we protected tools as we protect our limbs we would not be able to use them as extensively as we do, and the range of our actions would be far more limited.

Let us now consider the RHI. We saw in Section 1.3 that, in some cases at least, it does not impact reaching movements, but it has been found to modify protective behaviours. In one study, participants were in an immersive virtual reality system, which induced them to feel ownership over a virtual hand, which was then attacked with a knife. Although participants were instructed not to move, event-related brain potentials revealed a strong response in the motor cortex (González-Franco et al., 2013). This finding suggests that the RHI has a specific agentive mark in the context of self-protection.

To explain those results, we can propose that one has two functionally distinct body schemata, what we may call a working schema and a protective schema. The former incorporates tools, whereas the latter incorporates the rubber hand. They both consist in sensorimotor representations in direct connection with action, but their functions differ. The function of the working schema is to reliably covary with effectors in bodily contiguity and under direct control and to guide instrumental movements such as reaching and grasping. The function of the protective schema is to reliably covary with the body to protect and to guide defensive movements. As described by Colin Klein (2015a, p. 94) in his monograph on pain: 'Call this a defensive representation of the body: it shows which parts of the body are in need of which sorts of defence.' Studies in cognitive neuroscience investigate almost exclusively the working schema, neglecting the protective one, which plays a different role and which follows different principles. However, as we shall see in Section 3, the distinction between these two types of body schema can help us understand which body one experiences as one's own.

To conclude, I analysed here the relationship between bodily awareness and action. The standard treatment of this issue has been mainly proprio-centric,

---

[8] This does not mean that any object over which we have perfect control can be included in the body schema. Arguably, the cursor on the screen is not incorporated. One might then suggest that the body schema represents only effectors that are at least *contiguous* with the body (such as the fork held in the hand).

focussing on the role of proprioception for action guidance. However, the relationship takes a different form in protective contexts. The hypothesis is no longer that bodily awareness *guides* action but rather that it *motivates*, or initiates, action. We shall now switch from a conception of the body as an effector to a conception of the body as a motivating reason. To do so, we shall leave proprioception and turn to pain and to other affectively loaded bodily sensations, such as thirst and hunger, in order to assess their specific relation to protective agency.

2 The Affective Body

We scratch, we change posture to release muscle pain, we retrieve our foot from the water that is slightly too hot, we drink, we get some rest, and so forth. There is a sense in which our bodily experiences tell us what to do for the well-being of our organism, and their absence can have fatal consequences. Consider the case of patients with congenital insensitivity to pain. They have a dramatic impairment of nociceptive processing from birth and their lifespan is considerably affected because they are not alerted to bodily damage, even when severe, and they do not react as they should. Consider also adipsia following a lesion of the hypothalamus, which is characterized by the absence of thirst even in the presence of body water depletion or salt excess. It leads to severe dehydration because the patients no longer drink. There is thus a sense in which bodily awareness can be necessary for actions, or at least for some of them.[9] The way we protect our body is not based exclusively on reflex-like responses. It involves more complex behaviours (such as getting water), which are motivated by bodily experiences. The role of bodily experiences can then be *preventive* (e.g. avoiding being burnt), *regulatory* (e.g. maintaining the correct amount of fluid in the organism), and *restorative* (e.g. precluding certain types of movements in order to fix existing damage).

What drives the motivational force of bodily experiences is their affective phenomenal character. Their affectivity can be so pregnant that the boundaries between bodily experiences and emotions can be extremely thin. For instance, it is sometimes difficult to introspectively distinguish between the unpleasantness of pain itself and the unpleasantness of the anxiety caused by pain. Here we will consider pain, which is the classic example of affectively loaded bodily sensation, but also feelings based on interoception, such as hunger and thirst. Our discussion will be centred around three main issues:

---

[9] One might ask whether *fear of bodily damage* could suffice for protective agency, thus rendering bodily awareness unnecessary. However, one still needs to become aware of the danger for one to feel afraid.

(i)   What role does affective bodily awareness play for protective agency?
(ii) What kind of content enables affective bodily awareness to play this role?
(iii) Can one provide a unified account of affective bodily awareness?

2.1 The Motivational Role of Pain

The current working definition of pain provided by the International Association for the Study of Pain (IASP) is: ' An unpleasant sensory and emotional experience associated with, or resembling that associated with, actual or potential tissue damage.' One notable feature of this definition is that it assumes that pain cannot be reduced to the *perception* of bodily damage. It can indeed merely 'resemble' an experience caused by actual damage. Pain is typically based on peripheral signals sent by nociceptors (receptors that respond to potentially noxious stimuli), but it can occur independently of them. For instance, amputees who still experience the presence of their missing limb often describe acute pains in their phantom. No peripheral neural activity seems to be able to explain what they report but their pain is not conceived as being less 'real'. Likewise, individuals with somatoform disorders (i.e. chronic disorders for which no medical explanation has been found, such as fibromyalgia) often report chronic pain though there is no corresponding physical damage. The IASP does not draw a distinction between their pain and the pain that patients experience after physical damage.

Even when there are peripheral nociceptive signals, they rarely, if ever, get directly translated into pain. Instead, they are inhibited, enhanced, supplemented, or distorted via two gating mechanisms, one at the level of the spinal cord that controls the quantity of signals from the periphery to brain structures and one more central that modulates the intensity and the unpleasantness of pain by a range of affective and cognitive factors (Melzack and Wall, 1983). For obvious clinical reasons, most interest has focussed on the beneficial effects of positive expectations in placebo effects, but anticipating pain can also have detrimental effects, when one expects that it will worsen, leading to hyperalgesia (increase in pain sensitivity) and even to allodynia (pain response to non-painful stimulation) (Benedetti et al., 2003). It is not only one's judgement that is influenced by one's expectation but the sensation itself. Neuroimaging studies indeed show that pain expectation modulates activity in brain regions associated with pain (Wager et al., 2004). Hence, what one feels is influenced by what one expects to feel. Placebo and nocebo effects raise questions about the penetrability of pain to higher influences (Casser and Clarke, 2022; Gligorov, 2017; Shevlin and Friesen, 2021). However, little has been said about the nature of the anticipatory states that drive the effects. Some assume that they are doxastic (e.g. Shevlin and Friesen, 2021); others argue that they are affective (Benedetti et al., 2003). In the latter case, should placebo and nocebo effects still be conceived as instances of cognitive penetration? I shall leave this question open here and return to the IASP definition.

One may indeed wonder whether it is precise enough. For some individuals, seeing blood can be extremely unpleasant. One might claim in their case that their experience is both sensory and affective, that it has a negative valence, and that it is associated with actual tissue damage. It should thus qualify as an instance of pain according to the IASP criteria. Yet in these people their visual experience of their wound is unpleasant but not painful. Two elements appear to be missing in the IASP definition. It claims that pain is a 'sensory and emotional experience', but what is the relationship between these two dimensions, and how to characterize the emotional component itself?

First, one must distinguish within affectively loaded experiences those that are intrinsically bad, such as pain for instance, and those that are not. Let us return to the visual example. The mere sight of blood is generally devoid of affective character, and it can easily induce no response. When it is unpleasant, the unpleasantness is bound to the visual experience, but it seems to remain extrinsic to it. By contrast, it seems impossible, or at least exceptional, for pain not to feel bad and for one not to react to it. One might cite here the case of masochism as a counterexample, though one may argue that masochists feel good from feeling bad (see Klein, 2015a, chapter 13 for discussion). Another possible counterexample is the neurological condition of pain asymbolia (Bain, 2014; Grahek, 2001, Klein, 2015b). When exposed to noxious stimulations such as electric stimulations on the hand, asymbolic patients are able to judge the location and the intensity of the stimuli but they do not report what they experience as being unpleasant. Furthermore, their sensation does not seem to intrinsically motivate protective responses and they neither scream nor withdraw their hand. At first sight, one might conclude that these patients are in pain, but their pain is not unpleasant. This calls to mind Lewis's (1980) notion of mad pain: humans that show no reaction to pain.[10] Lewis then asks: do they have normal pain? Some reply negatively (Bain, 2014), others positively (Klein, 2015b). A shared – though controversial – assumption,

---

[10] Grahek (2001) also discusses the case of patients taking morphine, who still describe being in pain though they no longer complain about it. However, in their case, it has been suggested that morphine only relieves the second-order anxiety associated with pain, but that pain itself remains unpleasant (Price, 2000).

however, is that asymbolic patients no longer care about their own body (for discussion, see Vignemont, 2015).

The second way pain may differ from blood perception concerns the nature of the affective character. It is not clear that one can provide a unified account of unpleasantness across all domains, from the unpleasantness of seeing blood to the unpleasantness of pain, from the unpleasantness of hearing bad music to the unpleasantness of interoceptive feelings, and eventually to the unpleasantness of fear and other negative emotions. Even when focussing on pain, it has been noted that the sensation can greatly vary, from the piercing pain of a dental cyst to the pulsing pain of a headache, from the burning pain of stomach ache to the throbbing pain of a broken leg (Corns, 2020). There is also a variety of ways one can react to pain:

- Expressive (screaming 'ouch') versus protective (avoiding putting too much weight on one's twisted ankle).
- Body-directed (not turning one's head with a stiff neck) versus pain-directed (taking painkillers).
- Automatic (retrieving one's hand from the boiling water) versus reflexive (putting one's burnt hand under cold water).
- Passive (resting because of a headache) versus active (stretching to relieve back pain).

Are all these responses caused and motivated in the same manner by pain? Arguably, some of them do not require the organism to consciously feel pain. Unconscious nociception may be all that is needed. This issue plays a central role in discussions on animal pain, especially in species that do not have the brain structures known to be involved in pain in humans (Allen, 2004). But how to draw a line between behaviours for which unconscious nociception suffices and those for which pain is required? At first sight, it seems that nociception may be sufficient to trigger a narrow range of automatic protective movements limited in scope and flexibility, but that protective *agency* requires conscious experiences, including painful and emotional ones. In the agentive case, it is no longer the body taking care of itself but the subject doing so. These protective behaviours are said to be emitted, instead of triggered, because they involve the active engagement of the agent who decides what to do and when to do it. They recruit not only the motor system but also the executive system, and they require building more or less complex internal models of the situation, which can rely on direct past experiences, on extrapolation, and on reasoning (Ledoux and Daw, 2018).

What content, then, explains the motivational role of pain for protective agency under normal circumstances? Here, I consider two recent dominant views, evaluativism and imperativism, which have emerged in response to the difficulties faced by perceptualism (Armstrong, 1962). If pain perceptually represents bodily disturbance or damage, then pain content is partly similar to the visual content that one has when seeing one's finger cut, for instance. Yet one's pain and one's visual experience feel different, and they have different motivational force. To account for those differences, one may add evaluative content (Bain, 2013; Cutter and Tye, 2011): 'A subject's being in unpleasant pain consists in his (i) undergoing an experience (the pain) that represents a disturbance of a certain sort, and (ii) that same experience additionally representing the disturbance as bad for him in the bodily sense'[11] (Bain, 2013, S82). This characterization of pain is in line with a more general approach to emotions that accounts for affective phenomenal character in evaluative terms (e.g. Carruthers, 2018; Tappolet, 2016). However, many have questioned whether one could fully account for affective character on the only basis of evaluative content (Deonna and Teroni, 2012; Mitchell, 2021). In particular, it has been argued that, unlike sensory experiences, affective states are weakly opaque. Visual experiences are generally said to be diaphanous because when one turns one's introspection to one's visual experience of a cube, one is typically aware of the properties of the cube only and not of one's visual experience. The experience itself is transparent (Moore, 1903). By contrast, pain seems to be weakly opaque because when one introspectively attends to one's experience, one is not aware only of the badness of the damaged body part; one is also aware of something beyond that, of the special way one relates to the damage. The experience of pain itself is thus not fully transparent. One may then claim that pain is determined not only by its evaluative content but also by its experiential mode, under which one represents the damage. This special experiential mode could take the shape of a primitive negative attitude towards the bodily damage, akin to a sense of disfavour or dislike (Mitchell, 2021). The negative attitude may then explain why we frequently take painkillers. If pain simply informs us about something that is bad, getting rid of it seems as irrational as killing the messenger who carries bad news (Jacobson, 2013). Bain (2019) replies that, when in pain, one does not merely represent the disturbance as bad; one *perceptually encounters* its badness and this perceptuality is a crucial ingredient to explain why pain feels bad and why it can be an intrinsic motivating reason for pain-directed behaviour. However, it is not clear why this perceptual attitude makes the

---

[11] Something is bad in the bodily sense when it can harm one's body.

experience itself bad. By contrast, if one negatively experiences the bodily damage, it is easier to explain the badness of pain itself.

One may further wonder whether the evaluative content suffices to provide intrinsic motivating reasons for *body-directed* actions. Before defending evaluativism, Bain (2011, p. 179) suggested that pain content could 'inform us of what behaviour is such that, if it is not performed, injury will ensue'. One may then wonder about the direction of fit of pain content. As discussed in Section 1, one must distinguish between world-to-mind and mind-to-world directions of fit. If pain represents what to do, is its content exclusively descriptive or is it also directive? According to Millikan (1995), there is no need for information about motor possibilities if it is not for the motor system to exploit this information at one point. Consequently, she argues, the ultimate function of this type of representation is to guide actions. If Millikan's analysis is right, then pain has a world-to-mind direction of fit.

Such an approach to pain is in line with imperativism (Barlassina and Hayward, 2019a; Hall, 2008; Klein, 2015b; Martínez, 2011). According to imperativism, pain content does not evaluate the bodily situation but rather prescribes what to do about it. More specifically, the imperative content can be conceived as a form of bodily command that orders us to engage in protective behaviours. It is coercive: we must listen to pain, though we do not always do so. Its authority is benevolent: it normally – but not always – gives good advice: 'The imperatives that fix the affective phenomenology of our pains have the content they have because seeing to it that bodily damages disappear has been evolutionarily useful. This makes pain imperatives reliable guides to bodily health, and explains that it is typically reasonable to obey them' (Martínez, 2015, p. 2268). On this view, pain is not only a motivating reason that is part of the causal chain that leads to protective agency but also a justifying one that a rational agent would count as adequate. Pain can then be more or less intense and disrupt current courses of actions. According to Klein and Martínez (2018), the intensity of pain depends on the ranking of the imperative content compared to the pull of other conative states in action production. When the ranking is high, pain takes control precedence and the pain is intense.

The imperative view, however, has difficulty specifying the precise command that pain gives. First, is the content the same for all pains (e.g. 'don't have this bodily disturbance!') or does it depend on the type of pain and what causes it (e.g. 'do not put weight on this ankle!')? Generic accounts can be accused of failing to acknowledge the variety of pains: why do they all feel so different if they have the same content? On the other hand, pain-specific accounts have the reverse problem: why do all these experiences feel painful if they give different bodily commands? One may also object that pain content is not specific enough to distinguish it from the content of fear: 'But suppose you're on a cliff edge and have the urge not to step forward. If some urges are constituted by experiential commands, why not this one? And if this, why isn't it a pain?' (Bain, 2011, p. 178). A second issue concerns the target of the imperative: is it about the bodily state of affairs or about the sensation itself? One can distinguish two types of imperative content:

(i) Body-directed content: 'Don't have this bodily disturbance!'
(ii) Pain-directed content: 'Less of this pain!'

According to a first-order imperative account, pain has an imperative body-directed content (Martínez, 2011). According to a reflexive account, pain has an imperative pain-directed content (Barlassina and Hayward, 2019a). Finally, one must mention Klein's (2015a) two-layer account, which distinguishes between pain itself and painfulness, or what he calls suffering. On his view, painfulness is not constitutive of pain; it is a distinct attitude taken towards pain. Within this framework, he then defends a body-directed imperative account for pain (e.g. 'Don't put weight on your ankle!') and a higher-order imperative account for suffering ('Less of this pain!').

The reflexive account can easily explain why we take painkillers: 'when we experience pain, our first motivation is to get rid of the pain' (Barlassina and Hayward, 2019a, p. 12). The argument relies on the phenomenological insight that, when in extreme pain, one would do anything to make it stop simply because it feels awful (see also Bain, 2019). However, this description seems to better apply to feelings such as hunger than to pain. When we feel hungry, all we want is to no longer feel hungry. We are primarily concerned by the sensation itself and not so much by the amount of nutrients in our body. This is consistent with the reflexive conception (less of hunger!), but the situation seems to be different from pain, in which we are primarily concerned about the well-being of our organism. Barlassina and Hayward can reply that pain also intrinsically motivates body-related protective behaviours. The best way to stop pain is indeed to take care of the body. But is the motivation to stop the damage only secondary? It does not seem so. Barlassina and Hayward (2019b) claim to provide a unified account of all affective states, but it is already difficult to offer a unique explanation for the different types of pain. It is even more so if one wants to include other affectively loaded bodily sensations, and we should not overlook differences among them.

Furthermore, one may wonder about the evolutionary plausibility of the reflexive account. If pain represents 'Less of this pain', then it entails that the brain evolved a system whose only biological function is to self-extinguish. Martínez (2022) compares this hypothesis to Minsky's absurd idea of the

Ultimate machine: once turned on, it can only turn itself off. Instead, Martínez (2015) argues that we take painkillers because of the negative consequences of pain and not because of pain itself. Pain experiences are like inconvenient requests that we tend to block, especially once the bodily damage is taken care of, or if there is nothing that can be done. It is then rational to put a stop to the bodily command but only because it disrupts the ranking in action production for no good reason anymore. Hence, pain is intrinsically motivating exclusively for body-directed behaviour. For pain-directed behaviour, it is only extrinsically, or instrumentally, motivating.[12] Alternatively, one might say that it is suffering that intrinsically motivates pain-directed behaviours (Klein, 2015a).

2.2 Interoception, Homeostasis, and Bodily Urges

We now turn to interoception in order to determine whether one can apply the same principles as for pain. These last twenty years have seen an explosion of interest on interoception in cognitive neuroscience, though still very little in philosophy (Tsakiris and de Preester, 2018). Recent accounts have highlighted its role for emotions and decision-making but also for self-awareness, social cognition, and time perception. Surprisingly, however, there is little consensus on the definition of interoception (Ceunen et al., 2016; Leder, 2018). Sherrington (1906) introduced the term when giving his taxonomy of sensory fields. He first proposed a distinction between what he called the surface field and the proprioceptive field and then distinguished within the surface field the exteroceptive and interoceptive fields. It may seem surprising that interoception is a surface sense, but it should be clear that, for Sherrington, this did not entail that it covers only what happens on the skin. He exclusively referred to viscera (the large organs inside the thorax and abdomen, including the heart, stomach, lungs, kidneys, and intestines). By contrast, the proprioceptive field concerns the forces exerted in the depth of the body, in particular by muscles, tendons, joints and the walls of blood vessels.

Since Sherrington, many have adopted a more liberal definition, which includes within the scope of interoceptive awareness all sensations that have an affective component, including affective touch and pain, no matter whether they are located on the surface of the skin or inside. For instance, Craig (2010), one of the main experts on interoception in neuroscience, grounds his theory of interoception on the basis of a set of studies in which noxious stimulations are applied to various skin regions (e.g. on the lips, the wrists, and the hands).

---

[12] By contrast, according to Klein's two-layer account, pain itself intrinsically motivates only body-related behaviours, and it is suffering that intrinsically motivates pain-directed behaviours.

With such a liberal definition, one risks losing sight of the specificity of the sensory access that one has to one's internal organs. To add to the complexity, non-interoceptive signals often contribute to the way one is aware of the internal state of the body. Consider the sensation of feeling your stomach full after a nice meal. Here, interoceptive information is integrated with tactile information about the pressure on your skin. Interoceptive experiences are often multisensory, involving more than signals sent from interoceptors.

Even if we use Sherrington's narrower definition, one may question the homogeneity of interoception (Suksasilp and Garfinkel, 2022). We raised this point about pain, but the situation is even more extreme here. One can indeed distinguish several interoceptive axes, in which 'axis' denotes a specific organ system together with its peripheral innervation and central control mechanisms. Most research in cognitive neuroscience has focussed on the cardiac axis, but this is just a small part of the inner body, and when Sherrington first described the interoceptive field, he primarily referred to the visceral field and the alimentary function. The visceral field can itself be differentiated into the gastric axis, the intestinal axis, and the urinary axis. One can also add the respiratory axis. So far, each axis is associated with a specific internal organ, but interoception also covers physiological parameters that are not organ-based, such as thermal and hormonal information. If we apply Grice's (1962) criteria, originally proposed to individuate the external senses, we soon realize that there must be several *interoceptive senses*:

(i) *Properties that one is aware of*: Interoceptive signals carry information about rhythmic activity, energy, fluid concentration, temperature, pressure, tension, hormonal concentration, and so forth. Information about each property results from different types of computations and involves different types of regulatory mechanisms.

(ii) *Phenomenal character*: We are only rarely conscious of interoceptive signals, which is easily understandable given their quantity. When they give rise to conscious experiences, there seems to be no distinctive phenomenological signature shared by all interoceptive experiences (for instance, thirst and the sensation of one's heart beating too fast seem to have little in common).

(iii) *Physical stimulation*: The receptors are sensitive to different types of physical stimulation, such as mechanical, chemical, and hormonal.

(iv) *Sensory organs and internal mechanisms*: Interoception relies on a range of peripheral receptors, including mechanoreceptors, baroreceptors, thermoreceptors, and chemoreceptors. Neural responses also differ depending on the axis.

In light of this variety, one may ask to what extent one can draw conclusions about interoception in general from results concerning a specific bodily axis (Ferentzi et al., 2018). This methodological issue is especially important given the roles recently ascribed to interoception, from emotions to self-awareness. For instance, it has been shown that participants can be good at internally monitoring their gastric activity and their cardiac activity but not their respiratory activity (Garfinkel et al., 2016). Hence, one cannot directly compare the bodily axes. Furthermore, each bodily axis is difficult to experimentally investigate. One of the dominant paradigms involves asking participants to count their heartbeats to compute their 'interoceptive score', either directly on the basis of the reliability of their judgement or more indirectly by comparing the reliability of their judgement with the confidence that the participants have in it (Garfinkel et al., 2015).[13] Results show a massive variability among subjects, only a third being good at it. This measure, however, has been heavily criticized and leads to contradictory results (Brener and Ring, 2016). For instance, some studies suggest that anxiety traits are associated with heartbeat counting performance, but others find no correlation or even a negative one (Adams et al., 2022). Finally, one can note that the heartbeat score is devoid of any affective character and that it is disconnected from the primitive regulatory function of interoception. The heart functions well even in those who have a low interoceptive score. This score does not reflect the ability to maintain homeostasis.

Homeostasis is primarily about maintaining physical parameters of the internal milieu, including temperature, pH, and nutrient levels. *Homeostatic regulation* occurs purely internally (no need to act on the environment) and autonomously (with little or no voluntary control). For instance, heartbeat and respiration are accelerated when one is making a physical effort to supply muscles with oxygen. This is triggered by interoceptive signals about the chemical blood composition. The whole process can remain at a purely subpersonal level. Though one can decide to change one's respiration, most of the time it operates completely unconsciously and autonomously. According to Leder (2018, p. 213), it is 'when conscious awareness and volition are needed to aid in the preservation of bodily homeostasis' that interoceptive information reaches the threshold of consciousness. In other words, the need for protective agency would be at the origin of interoceptive awareness. Protective behaviours, then, involve planning sequences of goal-directed movements, which can be conceived as actions instead of mere physiological responses. For instance, feeling thirsty motivates you to go to the kitchen, open the fridge, take a fresh

---

[13] A more promising paradigm, but also more invasive, involves injecting different doses of isoproterenol, which is known to modulate the cardiorespiratory system, and measuring the participant's sensitivity to the changes using standard psychophysical methods.

bottle of water, go to the cupboard, take a glass, pour water in it, and eventually drink it. Your actions both alleviate your thirst (sensation-directed) and reduce the lack of liquid in your body (body-directed).

One may then be tempted to apply the same theoretical frame for pain and for interoceptive experiences:

- Evaluative view: Thirst consists in describing a bodily disturbance of a certain sort as bad for the subject in the bodily sense.
- First-order imperative view: Thirst consists in prescribing 'Don't have this bodily disturbance!'.
- Reflexive imperative view: Thirst consists in prescribing 'Less of this thirst!'.

Given the proximity in content with pain, one may wonder why thirst is generally not painful (though it might hurt in some extreme cases). Does it follow from the specific types of bodily disturbances or their degrees? Or are there more fundamental differences? Here, one may note that some interoceptive experiences are disembodied, so to speak. One says, 'I feel thirsty' and not, 'my body feels thirsty'. One might then argue that interoceptive experiences do not represent bodily disturbances; they only *respond* to them. They motivate primarily to appease the mind rather than the body. This would be in line with the reflexive account, but it is not clear that it can be generalized to all interoceptive experiences and in particular to positive feelings. Consider the feeling of satiety. It does not order us to have more of it. It rather urges us to stop eating. Because of their heterogeneity, it may be even more difficult to account for the motivational role of interoceptive experiences than for pain. Even a given interoceptive feeling such as thirst can motivate in multiple ways (Fulkerson, 2023).

One can draw several conclusions from this brief overview: (i) the primary role of interoception for bodily protection is at the physiological level of homeostatic regulation; (ii) only a minimal fraction of interoceptive signals leads to interoceptive experiences, which play a motivational role at the agentive level; (iii) interoceptive experiences are often multisensory, involving other sources of information; and (iv) interoceptive experiences differ in some major aspects from pain experiences. All together, these peculiarities question some of the conclusions drawn in the experimental literature about the role of interoception for cognitive abilities on the basis of interoceptive awareness only.

2.3 A Narcissistic Conception of Bodily Awareness

We have focussed so far on pain and interoceptive awareness, but one may argue that these are not the only bodily experiences that play a motivational role for protective agency. For instance, when you put your foot in the bathtub, you first feel that the water is too hot – though not painfully hot – and you retrieve your foot. Interestingly, if you decide to get into the bathtub, it feels less bad with time. In her description of thermal sensations, Akins (1996) argues that this is because your sensation is not about the precise temperature but about its safety for your organism:

> What the organism is worried about, in the best of narcissistic traditions, is its own comfort. The system is not asking, 'What is it like out there?', a question about the objective temperature states of the body's skin. Rather it is doing something – informing the brain about the presence of any relevant thermal events. Relevant, of course, to itself. (Akins, 1996, p. 349)

On her view, thermal sensations are not just servile detection systems that aim to be as reliable as possible in carrying information about the states with which they covary. Instead, they are concerned with the impact of what is perceived for the subject; they appraise whether or not the temperature is dangerous for the body given its thermal needs. They thus fulfil what she calls a narcissistic function.[14] The same could easily be said of pain and interoceptive experiences but also, one may suggest, of bodily awareness in general. It is indeed interesting to note that most bodily sensations that attract our attention have an affective value, whether positive or negative. It is often because the sensation of the cling of our shirtsleeve or the texture of our socks is concomitant with the breach of a certain threshold of comfort or discomfort that we notice it. Similarly, we rarely consciously experience the fine-grained details of the posture of our body unless it is highly uncomfortable or pleasantly relaxing. The case of the vestibular system is even more striking. We are completely unaware of our balance unless we suffer from vertigo or motion sickness.

There is a good reason for that. If the constant flow of bodily signals were conscious, our stream of consciousness would quickly become saturated. Even if one only concentrates on one's hands, the amount of information is overwhelming. The hands are one of the most sensitive parts of the body. Physiologically, they have the highest density of tactile receptors, which allows for fine prehension and discrimination in grasping. Add to this the fact that the hands are the preferred instrument for interacting with the world, and therefore most often in contact with it and in motion. Processing this constant flow of information is a real challenge for the brain, and if one were to be aware of it, there would be little room left for anything else. Imagine that you are typing a text message on your smartphone. What is more important, the exact position of your index finger or what you are writing? Unless we are learning a new skill,

---

[14] One may note that the term is badly chosen because, in the original myth, Narcissus ends up dying, while Akins's conception is primarily about survival.

such as playing the piano, the fingers must remain in the background of consciousness to make room for what matters, since the field of consciousness is limited and only what is most essential must be selected. Most of the time, this is not the body, which can perform well autonomously. Hence, though we constantly receive information about our body via several kinds of receptors and there may be no other object on which we receive as much information, the body stays silent for the most part. It is only when there is something with either a positive or negative value for the organism's comfort that we become aware of our body. Bodily sensations then alert us to the goodness or badness of our bodily states, and this in turn can motivate us to engage in protective behaviours.

One may wonder, however, whether the relationship between sensory and affective characters is the same for all bodily experiences. Indeed, one should not neglect major differences among the various types of bodily experiences. According to David Armstrong (1962), one must distinguish between local bodily *sensations*, such as the focal sensation of a pinprick at the fingertip, and global bodily *feelings*, such as the diffuse feeling of fatigue in the whole body. Within the category of bodily sensations, one must further distinguish between *transitive* and *intransitive* ones. In transitive sensations, as in touch, one experiences a mind-independent property (the pressure of the pen in the fingers), whereas intransitive sensations, such as pain, do not seem to provide awareness of states of affairs that exist independently of their being perceived. One may then note that in transitive sensations, the (un)pleasantness arises from the evaluation of the mind-independent property that elicits the sensation (e.g. the uncomfortable body posture), whereas in bodily feelings and intransitive sensations, it primarily characterizes the experience itself (e.g. the pleasant tickle). One may thus propose that it is only in the latter case that bodily experiences are intrinsically affective.

Now, one might believe that their narcissistic function prevents bodily experiences from being perceptual. Many have questioned the perceptual status of bodily awareness (Anscombe, 1962; Gallagher, 2003; Smith, 2002), but the debate has been especially vivid for pain, partly because it goes beyond the mere sensory registration of bodily damage (Aydede, 2005). However, Akins (1996) notes that all sensory systems are narcissistic. This theory of perception can already be found in Descartes (1641/1979): 'These perceptions of the senses, although given me by nature, merely to signify to my mind what things are beneficial and hurtful to the composite whole of which it is a part' (Descartes, 1641/1979, Meditation VI). A similar view can also be found in Malebranche (1674/1980): the senses do not represent 'immutable truths that preserve the life of the mind' but 'mutable things proper to the preservation of the body'.[15] More recently, it has been argued that the border between perception and emotion is more permeable that one might believe and that visual and auditory experiences can also be affectively loaded (Bergqvist and Cowan, 2018; Fulkerson, 2020; Jacobson, 2021; Vignemont, 2023). This seems to be confirmed by recent evidence in cognitive neuroscience showing that the visual system is influenced by the outcome of an early appraisal mechanism that automatically evaluates what is seen as being harmful or beneficial for the organism (e.g. Barbot and Carrasco, 2018; Maratos and Pessoa, 2019; Pourtois et al., 2013). It might then be that bodily awareness does not depart so much from perceptual awareness: they both fulfil a narcissistic function. In Section 3, we shall see how this narcissistic function is at the origin of bodily self-awareness. One may indeed propose that the narcissistic function of bodily awareness not only filters what bodily information to be conscious of; it also marks bodily experiences by highlighting their relevance *for the subject*: 'But how does this all relate to ME? … by asking the narcissistic question, the form of the answer is compromised: it always has a self-centered glow' (Akins, 1996, p. 345).

3 When the Body Becomes Mine

In the previous section, we saw how affective bodily awareness plays a crucial role for protective agency and thus for survival. Here, I shall propose that it also plays a crucial role for minimal self-awareness. Self-awareness is said to be minimal when it does not require linguistic ability or conceptual grasp of the first-person. It includes the sense of agency (awareness of oneself as acting) and the sense of bodily ownership (awareness of a given body as being one's own). At first sight, the former seems to be more important for instrumental agency and the latter for protective agency. Consider the following example. I raise my hand to ask a question. Here, what matters is that I am at the origin of the movement. It would not have the same implications if someone else had raised my hand for me. By contrast, it does not matter if it is my hand that I raise or a small hand symbol that I click on at a virtual conference. Compare now with the following situation. I withdraw my hand from the spider approaching. Here, what matters is that it is my own hand that moves away, but it does not matter whether the movement is active or passive. Only the safety of my own body counts, no matter how it is achieved. In brief, the sense of agency has often more cognitive significance when one positively interacts with the world, and the sense of ownership when one protects oneself from the world.

---

[15] For more details on Descartes and Malebranche, see Simmons (2008).

In this section, we shall explore this intuition further, focussing on bodily ownership. The sense of agency has been discussed extensively for several decades now, but the sense of bodily ownership has given rise to a large philosophical debate only more recently (Alsmith, 2015; Bermúdez, 2011, 2015, 2017; Billon, 2017; Bradley, 2021; Brewer, 1995; Dokic, 2003; Martin, 1995; Peacocke, 2017; Serrahima, 2023; Vignemont, 2018; Wu, 2023). We shall start by highlighting the challenges, both theoretical and empirical, that await any theory of the sense of bodily ownership. We shall then consider whether the sense of ownership can be solely explained by the spatial specificities of bodily sensations. We will see the limits of this sensory approach and defend an alternative conception according to which the sense of ownership consists in the affective awareness of the unique significance of the body for the subject's persistence.

3.1 The First-Personal Character of Bodily Awareness

When I report that I feel that my legs are crossed, there are two occurrences of the first-person. The first refers to the subject of the proprioceptive experience (*I* feel), and it reveals the subjectivity of the bodily sensation (what it is like *for me* to have my legs crossed). The second occurrence refers to the limbs that I feel being crossed (*my* legs), and this is what is at the core of the debate on bodily ownership. I can then judge that *my legs* are crossed and this self-ascription is said to be immune to error through misidentification relative to the first-person (Evans, 1982; Shoemaker, 1968): I cannot rationally doubt that those are my legs and nobody else's. Bodily immunity is only de facto: if the proprioceptive system were wired in a different manner, connecting me to other bodies, my proprioceptive judgements would not be immune; but in the actual world, my proprioception gives direct access only to my own legs.[16] Hence, there is no need to identify whose legs they are, and therefore no risk of misidentifying them. Judgements of ownership are thus immune when one experiences one's body from the inside. The crucial question is whether *bodily experiences* themselves are first-personal and, if so, in what sense. Here is a brief roadmap of three theoretical paths.

A first proposal consists in positing a primitive irreducible feeling of 'mineness' already at the experiential level (Billon, 2017). When I feel my legs crossed, not only do I proprioceptively represent their posture but I also represent them as belonging to me. On this view, mineness is represented not only at the conceptual level of my judgement but also at the non-conceptual level of my

---

[16] De facto immunity can be distinguished from absolute immunity, which is guaranteed by conceptual truths about the mental predicates that one self-ascribes.

bodily experience. The judgement simply endorses what is already presented in the sensation. This proposal offers an account for the first-personal character of the sense of ownership, but it seems to presuppose what it is supposed to explain. We can indeed ask: what grounds the mineness feeling?[17]

One can then adopt the opposite strategy and reduce the first-personal character to some non-first-personal features of bodily experiences (Bermúdez, 2017; Martin, 1995; O'Shaughnessy, 1980). In a nutshell, there is no individuation of the body that one feels as one's own if there is no discrimination from what is not one's body. This discrimination, however, should not be phrased in terms of self versus non-self to avoid a circular account of ownership. Instead, it can be phrased in spatial terms, between inside and outside boundaries in which one can locate bodily events. According to this reductionist approach, one experiences nothing more than somatosensory properties located in one's body, such as posture, temperature, pressure, and so forth, but these properties are experienced in such a way that one is necessarily aware that they are properties of one's body qua one's own. However, one may question this assumption. As Peacocke (2017, p. 292) notes: 'The content *this leg is bent*, even based on proprioception, or capacities for action with the leg, or both, is not yet the content *my leg is bent* . . . What more is required?' The challenge is to find a way to account for the transition from 'this leg' to 'my leg' without begging the question, one way or another. It is difficult to find a path that avoids the risk of giving either a circular account or no account at all. However, this may be possible if one explains the awareness of one's body as one's own (*my body*) by appealing to other types of experiential relation to the self, such as mental relation (the body that *I feel*), agentive relation (the body *under my control*), or affective relation (the body that *matters to me*). The overall hypothesis is that the sense of bodily ownership inherits, so to speak, its first-personal dimension from further sources.

How to settle the debate between these three options? Under normal conditions, introspection does not take us far, especially in the case of the body, which remains only marginally conscious most of the time. However, borderline cases in which the sense of bodily ownership becomes deviant can provide a unique insight into its origin. Consequently, most discussions have focussed on illusions of bodily ownership, in which healthy participants experience a fake body part as belonging to their own body, and on disownership syndromes, in which neurological and psychiatric patients no longer experience parts of their body as their own. As we shall now see, however, both raise methodological issues.

---

[17] For further objections to the mineness hypothesis, see Bermúdez (2011) and Vignemont (2020).

3.2 Methodological Challenges

The rubber hand illusion (RHI), which we described in Section 1, has been taken as the key to the scientific investigation of the sense of bodily ownership. As a reminder, participants sit with their arm hidden behind a screen while visually fixating on a rubber hand presented in their bodily alignment; both the rubber hand and the real hand are then stroked in synchrony or not (Botvinick and Cohen, 1998). Participants are asked to report on a scale whether it seems to them that the rubber hand was part of their body. It has been repeatedly found that some of them – but not all – rate significantly higher ownership towards the rubber hand after the synchronous stimulations than after the asynchronous ones. Another illusion that is interesting is the full-body illusion (FBI), which follows the same principle of visual capture of touch but with the help of a system of video cameras and virtual reality goggles. Participants see the back of a virtual avatar being stroked while feeling their own back being stroked (Lenggenhager et al., 2007). Some participants then report that it seems to them as if the virtual avatar were their own body.

Hundreds of versions of these ownership illusions have now been done but they have been recently criticized, with some claiming that they only test the participants' expectations about what they are supposed to report and not their experiences (Lush et al., 2020; for a reply, see Ehrsson et al., 2022). Part of the objection is based on the fact that participants can accurately describe what the illusion should feel like on the only basis of a verbal description of the RHI set-up (Lush, 2020). However, in a follow-up study, Lush and colleagues (2020) found that manipulating participants' expectations (by warning them before-hand what they should feel and when they should feel it) had no effect. Nonetheless, the authors concluded that the RHI 'requires' the contribution of top-down factors and that one can give a 'cognitive' account of the illusion (p. 6). Here, it is important to distinguish several claims:

(i)   The sense of bodily ownership can be causally influenced by cognitive states.
(ii) The sense of bodily ownership can be cognitively penetrated.
(iii) The sense of bodily ownership requires the contribution of cognitive states.

The results so far argue only in favour of the first claim. To find evidence of cognitive penetration, one needs to show that cognitive states can modify the way one experiences one's body independently of mere attentional effects. However, even if there were proof of cognitive penetration, that would still not suffice to show that cognitive factors are *necessary* for the sense of bodily ownership. Take the example of pain. Though it can be heavily influenced, including by expectations, very few are ready to claim that pain *requires* the involvement of top-down processes.

We have just seen that the interpretation of ownership illusions is not without controversies. So is the interpretation of disownership syndromes, which were discovered long before the RHI. One of the first cases was described in 1825: a patient said about the left side of his body that it felt 'as if it were a stranger to him; it seemed to him that somebody else's body was lying on his side, or even a corpse' (Bouillaud, 1825, p. 64). Almost two centuries later, a patient suffering from somatoparaphrenia described his left hand as follows: 'I'm sure, it isn't mine, I don't feel it as my hand' (Cogliano et al., 2012, p. 764). Somatoparaphrenia is caused by a lesion of or an epileptic seizure in the right parietal lobe and it is often associated with motor and somatosensory deficits and spatial neglect, but the main symptom is the patients' denial that one of their limbs (often their left hand) belongs to them and their ascription of the limb to another individual. Another interesting case is the psychiatric syndrome of depersonalization. Patients with depersonalization experience abnormal bodily properties (e.g. distorted body parts), and they feel detached from their body, feeling as though it does not belong to them or it has disappeared. For instance, a patient reports: 'I can sit looking at my foot or my hand and not feel like they are mine' (Sierra, 2009, p. 27). Xenomelia (also called body identity integrity disorder) brings the sense of disownership to its more fatal consequences. Patients have apparently normal sensory and motor functions, but since childhood or early adolescence, they describe that their limbs – often the legs – do not feel that they belong to their body and that they have an overwhelming desire to have them amputated. By analysing what is missing in all these disownership syndromes, one may shed light on the necessary grounds for the sense of ownership. Beforehand, however, one must question the validity of the method that uses pathological cases to understand normality.

First, should one take these patients at their word when they report that part of their body *feels* alien? The patients may report what they erroneously *think*, and not what they experience (Alsmith, 2015). This interpretation, however, does not appear likely in the case of depersonalization, and even less so in xenomelia, in which patients remain aware that their limbs belong to them. It only feels to them *as if* these limbs were alien. Could the mere thought that their legs are not parts of their body suffice to lead some of them to ask for amputation?

Alternatively, one may grant that the patients *experience* their limb as alien but deny that one normally experiences ownership feelings. The sense of ownership is indeed phenomenally elusive, whereas the sense of disownership is relatively vivid. One may then take this phenomenological asymmetry as evidence that there is an experiential component to the sense of disownership but not to the sense of ownership (Chadha, 2018; Bermúdez, 2011). This asymmetry, however, can be easily explained by a phenomenon of habituation. Since our body never leaves us, it becomes almost phenomenally transparent; but as soon as the situation becomes unusual, whether we feel estranged from our limb or acquire a new one, it quickly becomes more salient. As a soldier who had his leg amputated during the US Civil War claimed about his phantom leg: 'I am more sure of the leg which ain't than of the one that are' (Mitchell, 1871, p. 566).

Another way to conceive the relation between ownership and disownership is as two end points on a continuous spectrum. On this view, ownership is not a discrete property; it comes in degrees (Billon, 2023). This could explain the heterogeneity in disownership experiences. It could also explain the rating that participants in RHI studies give on quantitative scales (from −3 to 3, for instance). However, it is hard to conceive that a hand could belong to a certain individual to varying degrees. It rather seems that it is either her hand or not. If the function of the sense of ownership is to systematically covary with the metaphysical fact of bodily ownership (Dokic, 2003), then it should also be a matter of all or nothing. What can be graded is the vividness of the phenomenology, which depends on attentional and emotional factors. What can also be graded is the confidence associated with one's judgement. It would not be surprising that participants in RHI studies are only mildly sure that the rubber hand seems to be their own hand.

To conclude, one should keep in mind the disagreements on the exact interpretations of ownership illusions and disownership syndromes. Nonetheless, they provide an interesting window into the grounds of the sense of bodily ownership. We shall now discuss what conclusions we can draw on their basis.

3.3 The Sensory Approach

In line with O'Shaughnessy (1980), Martin (1992, 1995) and Bermúdez (2011, 2015, 2017) provide a deflationary account of the sense of bodily ownership that does not require positing additional properties beyond somatosensory ones (e.g. posture, motion, contact, temperature, and possibly disturbance) and their ascribed location within the body. On this view, the sense of ownership is 'somehow already inherent within them' (Martin, 1995, p. 278). This conception can be articulated into three complementary claims:

(i)   Phenomenological claim: When one feels sensations in a body part, one cannot but feel this body part as one's own.

(ii) Spatial claim: One locates bodily events within a bounded connected volume.

(iii) Metaphysical claim: Bodily awareness has a unique object, namely one's own body.

The phenomenological claim starts with the intuition that bodily sensations are felt to be located within the boundaries of one's own body and concludes that the sense of ownership depends on their spatial content: 'This sense of ownership, in being possessed by all located sensations, cannot be independent of the spatial content of the sensation, the location of the event' (Martin, 1995, p. 277). The spatial claim then explores the spatial organization of bodily awareness and determines the specific features in virtue of which the spatial content of bodily experiences can ground the sense of ownership. Bermúdez (1998) highlights two main characteristics. First, boundedness: 'Bodily events are experienced within the experienced body (a circumscribed body-shaped volume whose boundaries define the limits of the self)' (Bermúdez, 1998, 124); Secondly, connectedness: 'The spatial location of bodily events is experienced relative to the disposition of the body as a whole' (Bermúdez, 1998, 126). The phenomenological and the spatial claims, however, do not suffice on their own. The core of the sensory conception lies in the metaphysical claim, what Martin (1995) calls the sole-object view. The ultimate explanation of the sense of bodily ownership lies outside the spatial content of bodily experiences, in the identity between one's own body and the body that one perceives from the inside. Sensations that are felt beyond the actual limits of one's body, as in the case of phantom limbs or the RHI, should be conceived as hallucinatory or illusory. Hence, they do not pose a problem for the metaphysical claim. For a bodily experience to count as an instance of perception, it must indeed be an experience of what is in fact the subject's actual body. There cannot be veridical bodily experiences that do not fall within the limits of one's own body. It is because of this fact that the spatial phenomenology of bodily experiences is said to suffice for the sense of bodily ownership.

Many have questioned the sensory approach (Billon, 2017; Dokic, 2003; Peacocke, 2017; Serrahima, 2023; Vignemont, 2018). The objections can be grouped along two lines. The first targets the reductionist project of the sensory approach. Can one reduce self-awareness to spatial awareness? It seems difficult, if not impossible, to explain the first-personal character of bodily awareness on the only basis of its spatial features. Arguably, one can be aware of the boundaries of one's body without being aware of the boundaries of one's body qua one's own.

> For, we could still ask: on what grounds does the subject take the body at one
> of the sides of the boundary … to be her own in the relevant sense, while
> taking the object on the other side … not to be hers? Why should either side
> of the perceived boundary have the special import it has? (Serrahima, 2023,
> p. 259)

The bodily space may coincide with the space of one's own body, but this does
not entail that one is necessarily aware of this coincidence. The difficulty is that
the source of self-referentiality must be outside bodily experiences, but how
does one have access to it? From one's viewpoint, all that is presented is
a bounded volume in which various events happen.

The second objection specifically targets the phenomenological claim. At the
rational level, one cannot doubt that the body in which one feels sensations belongs
to oneself, but Martin (1995) claims that it is also true at the experiential level: one
cannot experience pain in a body part that does not seem to belong to one's body.
However, this assumption is false. Contrary to Martin's prediction, there are
situations in which one feels sensations located in a limb that does not feel as
being part of one's body. For instance, disownership syndromes, such as depersonalization and xenomelia, are not associated with sensory impairments. Even in
the case of somatoparaphrenic patients, who are fully convinced that their hand
does not belong to them, a metanalysis reveals that somatosensory deficits are
frequent but not systematic (95 per cent of the patients in Romano and Maravita,
2019). Some patients can feel tactile and painful sensations that they locate in their
'alien' limb. They can also accurately judge the position of their 'alien limb'. One
cannot simply reply that these sensations are abnormal unless one can explain in
what sense they are without begging the question. For instance, one should not
claim that sensations are normal only if one feels them to be located in one's body
qua one's own. On the contrary, if by normal sensations one means reliable
perceptions of somatosensory properties, then sensations in 'alien' limbs can
qualify as normal. For instance, some patients with somatoparaphrenia reliably
experience pressure when a tactile stimulation is applied to their 'alien' hand
(Moro et al., 2004). Another patient was able to reach her 'alien' hand with the
contralateral one, showing preserved proprioception (Romano et al., 2014).

Bradley (2021, p. 373) replies that these cases are not counterexamples to the
sensory approach because the sense of ownership is preserved at some fundamental level, as shown by the fact that the patients still have first-personal
capacities, such as 'motivation, withdrawal reflexes, protective dispositions,
etc'. However, his notion of ownership seems so minimal that one may wonder
whether it corresponds to the type of self-awareness that most philosophers
have focussed on. Many animals display these abilities, and it is not clear that
they have any degree of self-representation, even the most minimal one.

To conclude, the sensory approach relies on the intuitive assumption of a necessary connection between one's own body and the place in which one feels sensations. It is true that the spatial organization of bodily awareness displays unique peculiarities, but one needs to make a further step to show that it suffices to ground the sense of bodily ownership. One may then be tempted to supplement the sensory approach with an agentive dimension (Baier and Karnath, 2008; Ma and Hommel, 2015; Peacocke, 2017; Vignemont 2007). There are many versions of this agentive approach, but let us focus here on the following basic account: one experiences as one's own the body in which one locates bodily sensations and which is under direct control. However, this hybrid account is problematic. Consider the case of tools. Arguably, one can feel sensations in them, as illustrated by Descartes's description of the blind man feeling the world at the tip of his cane. A recent study confirms that one can accurately localize contact on a wooden rod not only at its end but also at various points, just as is possible on the skin (Miller et al., 2018). Hence, tools seem to meet the sensory criterion of the sense of bodily ownership. They also meet the motor criterion. As described in Section 1, tool use modifies the way one moves, even for movements that have never been performed with the tool (Cardinali et al., 2009). Yet tools are typically not felt as parts of one's own body.[18] Conversely, the absence of bodily control does not suffice to induce disownership. It is true that somatoparaphrenia typically involves some more or less extreme motor impairments (97.5 per cent in Romano and Maravita, 2019), with patients frequently complaining about the uselessness of their 'alien' limb. However, many patients have peripheral or central motor deficits (because of focal hand dystonia, apraxia, delusion of control, or spinal cord injury) and they still experience their limbs as their own. Finally, participants in the standard version of the RHI report no agentive feelings toward the rubber hand (Longo et al., 2008) and their movements can remain insensitive to the illusion (Kammers et al., 2009). Hence, even if one agentively enriches the sensory approach, it still cannot account for the empirical data. We shall now consider a different way to enrich the sensory approach, by acknowledging the special value of bodily boundaries for the subject's persistence.

3.4 The Value of the Body

We have just seen that the sensory approach is built on the claim that bodily awareness has a sole object, that is, one's own body. The affective approach to the sense of bodily ownership is built on a different metaphysical assumption:

---

[18] Nonetheless, it is possible to elicit the equivalent of the RHI for a mechanical grabber after synchronous stroking (Cardinali et al., 2021).

a subject's body is the body on whose preservation the subject's continued existence depends. This characterization of the fact of ownership assumes a materialist conception of the subject, according to which subjects cannot survive in the absence of a material substratum. However, it does not have stronger commitments. In particular, it makes no claim about which body is necessary for the subject's persistence. It is thus compatible with both biological and psychological conceptions of personal identity, as long as they are materialist. According to the biological conception, sometimes referred as animalism, we are biological organisms and our persistence consists in the continuation of processes constitutive of biological life (e.g. Olson, 1997; Snowdon, 1991). On this view, the subject's body is his/her biological body. According to the psychological conception, as defended by Shoemaker (1976), the subject's body is the body whose movements fulfil the movements that the subject is trying to produce (i.e. volitional embodiment), but it needs not be the biological body he/she was born with. To illustrate his view, Shoemaker imagines that his cerebrum is transplanted into a different living body and that the resulting person turns out to be exactly like him psychologically. At the same time, the cerebrum-less organism is kept alive. He argues that he will be the resulting person, and not the brain-less organism, and that his own body will be the new one, and not the original one. Still, there needs to be *a body*, or some functionally equivalent device, for the subject to persist through time. This body is the subject's body.

According to the affective approach to the sense of ownership, the fact of ownership is determined by the value of the body for the subject's survival, and the sense of ownership represents the body that has this special value. Whether this value itself is determined biologically or psychologically, the function of the sense of ownership is to facilitate the protection and the preservation of the body that has this special value. Furthermore, in both conceptions, the sense of ownership has the same accuracy conditions. It is accurate if one experiences as one's own the body on which one's existence depends. When one experiences a given body as having a special value, one is thus normally entitled to judge that this is one's own body because under normal circumstances the body that matters in such a way is one's own body.

Nonetheless, the conception of personal identity that one defends has some implications for the sense of ownership. One may first wonder about the actual value of the current body in psychological theories, since it can be replaced by another. It may seem that there is less need to protect it and that self-concern should be primarily psychological. This is not an objection against the affective approach to the sense of ownership, but the diminished significance of the body that one has at time *t* may possibly reduce the evolutionary importance of the sense of bodily ownership. Still, it is interesting to note that Shoemaker's (1976) main example of paradigmatic volitional embodiment actually involves bodily protection: the subject's body is the body that runs away from the snake that the subject sees and that leads him/her to desire to be elsewhere.

The second point concerns the scope of what one can accurately experience as being part of one's body. According to the animalist account, only the animal's biological body can satisfy the sense of ownership and all the cases in which one experiences as one's own a limb that is not part of the animal's biological body, such as a prosthesis, count as errors of ownership. By contrast, according to Shoemaker's volitional account, there may be situations in which the sense of ownership is correct even if one experiences as one's own a body, biological or artificial, different from the one that one was born with, as long as it is necessary for one's persistence. The RHI remains an illusion since the rubber hand has no role to play for self-preservation, but if an amputee experiences a prosthesis as a part of his/her body, one might say that there is no error since the prosthesis is part of the body that is to be preserved.

3.5 Affective Awareness

To recapitulate, I argued that the sense of ownership is accurate if the subject experiences as his/her own the body necessary for his/her persistence. The sense of ownership can then be defined as the awareness of the spatial bodily boundaries as having a special value for the subject's persistence. It consists in a specific kind of *affective awareness*. To be clear, this affective awareness is not a consequence of the sense of ownership. I do not need first to experience this hand as my own for me to be affectively aware of its value for me. Instead, I am affectively aware of the value of the body for me, and this affective awareness is what it is to experience my body as my own.

The sense of ownership thus belongs to the larger category of *affective feelings*. It presents the body as having a special value for the subject in the same way as the feeling of familiarity presents a person, or a place, as having a special significance, the difference being the source of the significance. In one case, it is the fact that the subject's survival depends on this body; in the other, the fact that the person or the place is already known to the subject. In both cases, sensory and affective dimensions of awareness are intermingled. When one meets by chance a long-lost friend, one has a dual phenomenology, both visual and affective (Dokic and Martin, 2015). Likewise, the phenomenology of bodily awareness is normally dual, both somatosensory and affective.

What is then the representational ground of the sense of ownership? According to what I call the *bodyguard hypothesis*, I propose that one experiences as one's own the body that is represented in the protective schema (Vignemont, 2018). As a reminder, the function of the protective schema is to reliably covary with the body significant for well-being and survival. The affective approach acknowledges the importance of agentive abilities, but it narrows them down to abilities displayed in protective contexts. The protective schema answers two questions: (i) where does the body stop and the rest of the world start? and (ii) what matters for the subject's preservation? Arguably, in order to first set it up, there is a stage in development in which it is important, possibly even necessary, to experience pain. Consider the case of patients with congenital insensitivity to pain. As described in Section 2, these patients are born with a deficit of their nociceptive system. Though they have no other somatosensory, interoceptive, or motor deficits, their relationship to their body remains remote and detached. They even frequently engage in self-mutilation, burning or amputating their own fingertips and tongues (Danziger and Willer 2009). A patient, for instance, said: 'A body is like a car, it can be dented but it pops out again and can be fixed like a car. Someone can get in and use it but the body isn't you, you just inhabit it' (Frances and Gale, 1975, pp. 116–17). Unlike deafferented patients, this patient can proprioceptively guide his movements. Yet he seems to be lodged in his body like a pilot on a ship. I suggest that this is because his body has failed to acquire affective significance for him. In more cognitive terms, his protective body schema has not developed normally. The bodyguard hypothesis thus predicts that disruptions of the protective schema – congenital or acquired – should lead to disruptions of ownership. As we shall now see, this prediction is confirmed.

It has been found that when patients with somatoparaphrenia see their 'alien' hand under threat, they display no increase in skin response conductance (SCR), which is normally associated with arousal and anxiety (Romano et al., 2014). One may conclude that the 'alien' limb is no longer represented within their protective schema. Conversely, the RHI is associated with an increase in SCR when participants see the rubber hand under threat. The higher participants rate ownership for the rubber hand, the more they affectively respond to its being in danger (Ehrsson et al., 2007), and the higher the intensity of evoked potential response in the motor cortex, as if the brain was preparing for withdrawal (González-Franco et al., 2013). One may then suggest that participants experience the rubber hand as a part of their own body because it is represented in their protective schema. Finally, if we consider tools, I noted in Section 1 that one normally does not protect them in the way one protects one's body. One actually never feels pain in tools. One may then propose that one generally experiences no ownership towards tools because they are typically not represented in the protective schema.

We shall now consider a series of issues that the affective approach raises, starting with the fact that some patients with somatoparaphrenia can still experience pain in their 'alien' hand and negatively react to it (Maravita, 2008; Melzack, 1990). This is in contradiction with the sensory approach, but this may also seem to challenge the affective one if one takes the patients' response as evidence that their limb still has an affective significance. However, as argued in Section 2, one should distinguish body-directed and pain-directed behaviours. The patients' aversive reaction may well be only of the second type, motivated by their desire to have some relief from the pain itself. If so, their response does not necessarily entail that their 'alien' limb is represented in their protective schema. It only indicates that the sensation feels unpleasant. Still, one may reply, the pain that the patients feel should be able to re-establish the affective value of their 'alien' limb. This objection raises questions about the rules that govern the malleability of the protective schema. Arguably, multiple factors are in play, including affective factors among others. If some are missing, the presence of others may not suffice to recalibrate the bodily representation.

One may then ask about affectively loaded sensations other than pain. As described in Section 2, the affective character of bodily awareness is pervasive. In particular, one might expect interoceptive feelings, which are essential for self-preservation, to play a role for the sense of bodily ownership. Recent accounts of interoceptive awareness have indeed highlighted its importance for self-awareness, positing it at the core of what is sometimes called the 'proto-self' (Damasio, 1999), the 'embodied self' (Seth, 2013), or the 'material me' (Tsakiris, 2017). However, the relationship between interoception and self-awareness is complex. On the one hand, some interoceptive feelings make no mention of the body: I feel thirsty. On the other hand, one refers to one's visceral responses as something that one's internal organs do, and not as something that one does: my heart beats fast; I do not beat fast. Interoceptive awareness may thus provoke 'a sense of self-body dualism' (Leder, 2018, p. 310). Furthermore, self-awareness arises from the need to distinguish the self from the world. More specifically, the sense of bodily ownership involves being able to discriminate one's body from what is not one's body. Skin sensations are located at the border between the body and the world, and thus allow for such discrimination, but interoceptive awareness is deep inside, with no access to the outside, and thus no possibility to draw the boundaries of the body. Hence, interoceptive awareness seems to be of limited interest for the sense of bodily ownership.

A third issue concerns altruism. How can the affective conception explain that we protect many other bodies than our own and that we do not always protect our own body? The reply is simple: we should not take protective agency as being a unified category even when it is selfish. Compare the following two examples. You set aside some money to make sure you still have something to survive on when you retire. Or you slowly withdraw when the dog starts barking at you. In the first case, your behaviour results from complex decision-making, involving a variety of beliefs, desires, emotions, moral considerations, and so forth. At this level, you may give priority to other people's interests instead of yours. In the second case, your defensive action is primitive, and though it should not be confused with a physiological reflex, it is based on direct connection between perception and action. What you then protect is determined by what is represented in the protective schema, whose function is to exclusively represent the body that matters for your persistence (though it can misrepresent it, as in the RHI and in disownership syndromes).

To conclude, I have argued that the phenomenology of ownership has to be understood in affective terms. However, we saw in Section 2 the difficulty that one faces in accounting for affective phenomenal character. So far, I have assumed that bodily experiences have intentional content. Many have argued that intentional content exhausts phenomenal character, appealing to the argument from transparency (Moore, 1903), but this claim is already controversial for standard sensory experiences (Block, 1996), and it is even more so for bodily experiences. In particular, if the sense of ownership consists in the affective awareness of the significance of the body for the subject, one may wonder whether this affective awareness is best understood in terms of content or of experiential attitude. According to a content-based approach, bodily experiences have different content when one experiences ownership. By contrast, according to an attitude-based approach, bodily experiences can have the same content in both cases but under different experiential modes. This latter path has yet to be explored.

4 When the World Is Here

What has become apparent throughout this Element is that bodily awareness cannot be understood without reference to the awareness of the outside world. They are like two facets of the same coin, one spatially individuating the other and vice versa. Their connection can be articulated at three levels.

First, we cannot represent bodily boundaries if we do not represent that there is something beyond the body. We are aware that there is a larger space in which our body is just one object among others, and this gives us the sense of our own boundaries. Secondly, the sense of a larger space gives us information about where we stand in the world. We represent the location of the surrounding objects in relation to bodily location and, conversely, we represent bodily location, and possibly self-location, in relation to the perceived objects. Finally, the sense of being in a larger space gives us reasons to act. Instrumental agency aims at exploiting the resources provided by the external world, whereas protective agency aims at defending us from threats, many of them coming from the outside.

In this section, we shall analyse the articulation between egocentric awareness and bodily awareness, at both close and far range, in physical and virtual environments. In my office, I can see the door on my right, the bookshelf in front of me, and the window on my left. In what sense do these egocentric experiences qualify as being first-personal? They locate objects relative to me, but am I part of their content? Do they require the ability to locate myself, or more simply, to locate my body? We will further ask whether egocentric experiences represent space uniformly. One might believe that the only spatial divide is between the body and the rest of the world. On this view, one experiences all objects as being 'out there', whether it is the door on the right or the moon in the sky, distinct from 'here', the place from which one sees them (Eilan, McCarthy, and Brewer, 1993; Richardson, 2017). However, I will show that there is a region of this outer space, known as peripersonal space, that has a unique relevance for the subject and in which perception is in direct relation with action. I shall argue that it constitutes a bridge between the body and the rest of the world.

4.1 Egocentric Experiences

Perceptual experiences are perspectivally structured. I see the world from somewhere and the point of origin of this particular perspective, which Husserl (1952/1989) calls the zero point, is where I am located. Visual experiences are structured according to this egocentric perspective: I locate objects on the basis of their spatial relation along various axes that are centred on me (up–down, left–right, front–back). This in turn allows me to locate myself in relation to these objects.

> Consider ... the everyday case in which an ordinary person forms a belief with the content 'I am in front of a door', and does so for the reason that he sees a door ahead of him. His visual experience represents the door as bearing a certain spatial relation to him. This is so even if he cannot see or otherwise experience his own body on this particular occasion. It would still be true that, taking his experience at face value, he would judge that he is in front of a door. (Peacocke, 2000, p. 264)

On the basis of egocentric contents, I can judge that I am at a place that is in front of a door, for instance, or in front of a tree, and, as noted by Evans (1982, p. 222), I cannot have the following doubt: 'someone is standing in front of a tree, but is it I?' Evans concludes that egocentric experiences guarantee the immunity to error relative to the first-person of self-locating judgements. They can also ground judgements about one's bodily movements, in what is known as visual kinesthesis: one can experience that one is moving solely on the basis of self-specific invariants in the optical flow (e.g. rapid expansion of the entire optic array). Visual kinesthesis is well illustrated by the 'moving-room' experiment: participants are placed in a room whose walls and ceilings can be made to glide over a solid and immovable floor. Since they cannot see their feet or the floor, it can suffice for them to see the walls moving backward and forward to experience themselves as moving back and forth. They can ask, 'Am I really moving?', but it does not make sense for them to ask, 'Am I the person that I experience moving?'. Even though their judgement is based on vision, they do not need to identify the person who is moving and their judgement is thus immune to error through misidentification of the first-person (Bermúdez, 1998). Visual information about the environment can thus be a legitimate ground for self-knowledge. The following two questions then arise:

(i) Does egocentric visual content represent the self?
(ii) What grounds egocentric visual content?

Let us first analyse what egocentric experiences represent. They represent the door, the tree, the walls, or whatever the subject sees. Since these perceptual objects are experienced in their spatial relation to the subject, is the subject himself/herself also perceived? Evans (1982, p. 232) replies negatively: 'A subject can know he is in front of a house simply by perceiving a house. Certainly, what he perceives comprises no element corresponding to "I" in the judgment "I am in front of a house": he is simply aware of a house'. Vision can convey information about the self, but the self is not an object of perception. The crucial question is whether perceptual content represents only objects of perception. According to Peacocke (2016), there is more in perceptual content than what one perceives. The content is fixed by its truth conditions. Since the truth of the visual content <the house is in front> depends on my location, the visual content is said to represent my location: it represents that the house is in front of *me*. Even if I do not see myself when I see the house in front, the self is still part of the visual content. This view is known as the self-location thesis (Cassam, 1997; Peacocke, 2000; Schwenkler, 2014): 'In ego-centric spatial perception the objects of perception are experienced as standing in spatial relations to the perceiver ... in experiencing objects as spatially related to one, one literally experiences the bodily self as located in the perceived world' (Cassam, 1997, pp. 52–3)

Many reject the self-location thesis (Alsmith, 2017; Campbell, 2002; Evans, 1982; Perry, 1993; Richardson, 2017). Campbell (2002), for instance, argues that egocentric terms should not be conceived as referring to relational properties between the perceived object and the self (e.g. in front *of me*) but rather to monadic properties (e.g. in front). Perry (1993) also argues that the first-person can remain implicit, or what he calls unarticulated. At the linguistic level, we often do not specify what is obvious from the context. For instance, when I tell you, 'it is noon', I do not explicitly articulate in what time zone it is noon. According to Perry, mental contents follow the same principle. They do not explicitly represent what can be directly extracted from the context. In the case of egocentric experiences, one may propose that the first-person can be extracted from structural features of the visual field, such as its sensory limitations (when focussing on one point, there are locations in which one cannot see objects) (Richardson, 2017). This would explain how the first-person can remain unarticulated.

The debate on self-location partly results from fundamental disagreements about perceptual content. Nonetheless, some have hoped to settle it with the help of the method of phenomenal contrast. The method works as follows (Siegel, 2010). One starts with the hypothesis that the visual content represents a target property (the first-person in this case). One then considers a pair of experiences that differ phenomenally, with one representing the property and the other not representing it. One then determines whether the target hypothesis is the best explanation of the phenomenal contrast by ruling out alternative explanations. The problem is that the method has led to opposite conclusions about egocentric content (Alsmith, 2017; Schwenkler, 2014).

Another way to reply to our question may be to assess to what extent egocentric content requires self-representational abilities. Do I need to be able to represent my location when I visually experience my keys as being right here? Or could there be a selfless notion of here, independent of any first-personal abilities? According to Peacocke (2014), a creature with what he calls a 'degree zero' of self-representation can still refer to its location in a mental map of its surroundings:

> None of its perceptual states have *de se* contents of such forms as that thing is that direction from me. Rather, they have here-contents, such as that thing is that direction from here . . . Its map has, so to say, not a *de se* pointer I am here, but rather one saying this place on the map is here. (p. 30)

There is a cost to pay for such a selfless here-notion, however. According to Peacocke, the creatures devoid of first-personal abilities could display only physiological changes (such as change of colour or release of chemicals), but no bodily movements: 'The case as described does sever any tight connection between the presence of spatial content in perception and spatial bodily action by the creature' (p. 31). Peacocke's assumption is that, in the absence of self-representational abilities, 'here' is disconnected from action (Schwenkler, 2014; Taylor, 1964). It is often assumed that first-personal, or *de se*, attitudes cannot be replaced by any other attitudes without running the risk of losing their cognitive significance. This has been well illustrated by Kaplan's (1989) famous example. I see in a window the reflection of a man whose trousers appear to be on fire. If I believe it under the character 'The man's trousers are on fire', I behave very differently than I would if I believed it under the character 'My trousers are on fire'. Likewise, one may propose that I can immediately grasp the keys when I see them as being here only because I represent that I am at the location where the keys are. However, the necessity of the first-person for action is controversial (Cappelen and Dever, 2013; Millikan, 1990). One can form the intention that a certain state of affairs obtain, for instance that a certain door is closed, and the intention may trigger the action to open it without the need of any self-referential attitude, such as a *de se* intention of the type 'I walk to the door and turn the doorknob'. In this example, the first-person is not required for action. One can also note that most animals display protective behaviours whose complexity can go beyond the mere release of chemicals. Yet do they all have self-referential abilities? Consider the example of fruit flies. Their flight responses triggered by the detection of looming visual stimuli are influenced by the size of the stimulus (Tammero and Dickinson, 2002). They are clearly beyond physiological reflexes. But do the fruit flies need to represent their self-location to fly away? This seems hardly likely. All they need is to represent 'danger here', where 'here' can be understood independently of self-reference. Interestingly, Peacocke (2016, p. 352) himself later acknowledges that he was maybe 'much too timid' in his early characterization of what selfless creatures could do and that their abilities could far exceed what he originally thought. One may then propose that there is a here-notion that makes a significant contribution to action independently of the first-person. The question then becomes: what grounds such a notion?

4.2 Bodily Anchoring

Evans (1982, p. 153) rightly notes, 'It is true that <p=here> is the same thought as <I am at p>; but this does not mean that I identify *here* as *where I am*'. According to his dispositional account – described in Section 1 – one can perceive a place as 'here' in virtue of one's dispositions to act towards the objects that occupy the place (Brewer, 1992; Briscoe, 2014). Though these dispositions can involve many different types of movements, there is a unique behavioural space common to all sensory experiences. One can then identify 'here' by locating the centre of behavioural space – the origin of one's perception and action – without appealing to any first-personal component.

> The interrelation between perception and action constitutes a kind of triangulation of the subject's location in the single world of each. Neither of these capacities alone, that is to say neither perception nor action, suffices to permit the subject to form a representation of his place in the objective world. It is rather that his self-location depends upon the interrelations between his perceptual experience and his purposive interaction with the perceived environment. (Brewer, 1992, p. 27)[19]

'Here' then refers to the place from which one can perceive and act. On one interpretation, this place is one's body. It is indeed the body that anchors one's capacities to perceive and that makes action possible. To be clear, the proposal is not that one needs to first represent which body is one's own in order to determine which space should be represented as here. This would bring back a first-personal component ('here' would refer to the space anchored on one's body qua one's own), which we are trying to explain away. The claim is only that the body can be taken as the zero point from which one perceives and acts on the world. Self-location is reduced to body-location.

A difficulty arises with the case of out-of-body experiences (OBEs), in which the origin of perspective does not coincide with the body. OBE results from vestibular dysfunction in addition to a disruption of multisensory integration (Lenggenhager and Ho, 2022). Individuals with OBE report seeing their body and its environment from an elevated viewpoint *outside of their physical body*: 'I was in bed and about to fall asleep when I had the distinct impression that "I" was at the ceiling level looking down at my body in the bed. I was very startled and frightened; immediately [afterward] I felt that, I was consciously back in the bed again' (Irwin, 1985, in Blanke and Arzy, 2005, p. 16). On the basis of OBE, what can we conclude about the zero point from which we perceive the world? First, it does not need to be embodied. In OBE, perceived self-location does not coincide with perceived bodily location. It is important here to distinguish OBEs from autoscopic hallucinations (i.e. visual experiences of one's own body from the outside). In both cases, one visually experiences one's body in external space, but in autoscopic hallucinations one does not feel outside of one's body. Instead, the seen body is experienced as that of a double. Hence, one's viewpoint remains embodied. By contrast, in OBEs, there is a unique

---

[19] See Schellenberg (2007) for a similar account and Alsmith (2021) for discussion.

body, the one seen from the outside, and one's viewpoint is disembodied. Interestingly, it seems that with the lack of embodiment comes also impoverished agency. In most clinical reports, both the body in bed that the patients see and their 'elevated self' remain still. According to Metzinger (2005), patients with OBEs only have the ability to voluntarily control their attention but not to act on their environment. The connection between perception and action is severed. One may then wonder to what extent this almost purely sentient disembodied viewpoint should be taken as a model of the way we normally visually experience the world. Hallucinations and perception do not have to follow the same principles, even if they can be introspectively indistinguishable.

The full-body illusion, in which participants can see their body from the outside, does not offer clearer answers. With a system of video cameras and virtual reality goggles, participants have the illusion of seeing their back being stroked, as if they were behind their body, while feeling at the same time the tactile sensations on their back (Lenggenhager et al., 2007). When the stimulations are synchronous, they report that it seems to them as if they could see their body from the outside, as in OBE. However, it is not clear whether the ownership that the participants experience towards the virtual body is associated with a complete disownership of their own body. In other words, their viewpoint may still be embodied. In this sense, the illusion is more similar to autoscopic hallucinations than to OBE.

A possibly more promising source of insight comes from studies of immersion in virtual reality (VR), which have the advantage of manipulating egocentric awareness and bodily awareness in fully controlled paradigms. One of the main challenges in VR is to induce the impression that one is 'there', present in the virtual environment. In VR, the notion of presence refers to behavioural and phenomenological responses to the degree of immersion of the technology. One can distinguish two main aspects: the impression of 'being in the place depicted by the VE [virtual environment]' (Slater, Spanlang, Sanchez-Vives et al., 2010, p. 92) and the impression of 'what is apparently happening is really happening' (p. 92).[20] They correspond to two distinct illusions that can come apart, known as the place illusion and the plausibility illusion.

One of the interesting features of VR is that it allows comparing embodied and disembodied visuospatial perspectives. In a series of studies by Slater and collaborators, participants saw the virtual environment from a first-person perspective. In one condition, they could see some body parts of a virtual avatar

---

[20] For a similar distinction within the sense of presence outside of VR, see Dokic and Martin (2017).

with the viewpoint that they would have for their own body (e.g. the avatar's hands, legs, and feet from a first-person perspective). In the other condition, there were no virtual body parts to see. The participants might still have a sense that they had a body, but they did not see it where they expected it to be. In this sense, it may be said to be quasi-disembodied. The results showed that the place illusion and the plausibility illusion were at their highest in the embodied set-up and when the avatar was under control (Slater, Spanlang, and Corominas, 2010).[21] In a post-experiment debrief, 90.9 per cent of participants said that seeing the virtual body from the first-person was the most important factor in improving their sense of presence in the virtual environment (Skarbez et al., 2017). Embodiment can thus be conceived as essential – possibly necessary – to anchor oneself in a given environment, whether real or virtual. We shall now see that bodily anchoring takes a special form in the perception of one's immediate surroundings.

4.3 Fractioning the Outer World

According to the dispositional account, the spatial distance between the subject and what is seen is not relevant. For instance, it is sufficient to be poised to turn one's head towards an object for it to be part of one's behavioural space. The moon up in the sky can thus be part of one's behavioural space. However, it makes a difference if one considers the notion of behavioural space from the perspective of self-preservation. Consider a threat, such as a snake, seen twenty metres away or next to one's foot. There is a sense in which only in the latter case does one see it as being 'here'. Only then indeed does one represent it as possibly being at the location of one's body in an immediate future. Within behavioural space, we can isolate a small fraction that immediately surrounds one's body parts (typically up to 50 cm), what is known as *peripersonal space*. It may be conceived as a grey zone between the body and the outer world.

Before entering into the details of the peculiarities of peripersonal space, let us first distinguish it from two related notions. The first is what is known in the literature as *personal distance*. It was introduced by Hediger (1955), the director of the Zurich Zoo, to describe the distance at which the presence of other animals is tolerable. In humans, it is measured by the feeling of discomfort triggered by what can be felt as an intrusion by another individual. Hediger contrasted this with social distance, at which one needs to be to belong to a group. Later, the social psychologist Hall (1966) drew more distinctions:

---

[21] As with the sense of bodily ownership, one may ask whether there are degrees of sense of presence or whether the rating in questionnaires corresponds to degrees of confidence.

intimate space, in which one can feel the warmth of another person's body (up to 45 cm); personal space, in which one can directly interact with another individual (between 45 cm and 1.2 m); social space, in which one can work with others (between 1.2 m and 3.6 m); and public space, in which one has no social relation. Unlike personal space, the notion of peripersonal space does not have only a social dimension. It refers to the proximity of other agents, but also of objects. A more closely related notion is known as *reaching space*. It is functionally defined as the distance at which an object can be reached by the subject's hand without moving his/her trunk (up to 1 m) (Delevoye-Turrell et al., 2010). Peripersonal space and reaching space are often confused for each other, but they display different properties and can be experimentally dissociated (Zanini et al., 2021). The extent of peripersonal space is generally smaller than that of reaching space; and instead of being anchored around the arms only, it surrounds several parts of the body, including the head, the torso, the hands, and the feet. Furthermore, though they have both been described as the space in which one acts, reaching space covers only a narrow range of movements, those that are instrumental and that are performed by the upper limbs. By contrast, peripersonal space also plays a role in protective agency. Along with the protective schema, it is one of the neural tools that the brain evolved for self-defence. One may reply that, if an approaching threat is 30 cm away from the body, it is already too late. Clearly, one does not wait until the last minute to be ready for a lion attack. Nonetheless, peripersonal space is adaptive because things rarely go as planned. There are many events that one can fail to anticipate correctly or that are expected but for which one's responses are not successful. In these circumstances, peripersonal space is the last resort.

How, then, does peripersonal perception (i.e. perception of peripersonal space) operate (for details, see Vignemont et al., 2021)? A first defining feature is that one allocates more attentional resources to one's immediate surroundings. Perception must be especially thorough in peripersonal space because partial overlook can be immediately dangerous. What is close can indeed be a direct threat. Hence, one can afford not to look at all the objects in a faraway visual scene but one needs to watch closely where one puts one's hand or one's foot. One should not believe, however, that peripersonal perception is only a matter of attention. What makes it unique is the multisensory mechanisms that it involves. Many of our perceptual experiences result from interactions among multiple sensory modalities (O'Callaghan, 2019), but what is special about peripersonal space is the type of interaction: information from external senses (vision or audition) impacts bodily senses (touch or pain). More specifically, the perceptual system predicts that external events in one's immediate surroundings can soon become bodily events: objects that are for now only *close to* the body could soon be *on* the body. This could be because one moves and the movement then unfolds within peripersonal space. It could also be because an object is looming towards one's body. In order to be prepared for the forthcoming contact, tactile expectations are generated on the basis of visual experiences. At the neural level, it has thus been shown that neurons in the ventral premotor areas in monkeys that are normally activated by tactile stimuli on the body are also activated by visual stimuli if presented in the space close to the body (Rizzolatti et al., 1981). At the behavioural level, these last twenty years have revealed a range of visuo-tactile and auditory-tactile effects that occur only when the visual or auditory stimulus is presented in the immediate surroundings of the body. For instance, one is slower and makes more mistakes in judging the location of tactile stimuli if, at the same time, one sees a visual stimulus close to the body but at a location that is incongruent with the tactile loci (Spence et al., 2004). In other words, the perceptual system anticipates the potential impact of what is seen, thus generating tactile predictions, which can then compete with the experience of the actual tactile stimulus. Interaction of this type does not occur when visual stimuli are presented further away. Objects located in peripersonal space are thus encoded not only within an egocentric frame of reference but also within a somatotopic, or bodily, frame of reference, exploiting the same frame as touch and pain. In the same way I feel touch on my hand, on my foot, or on my head, I can see objects in my peri-hand, in my peri-foot, or in my peri-head. Graziano (2018), one of the leading experts on peripersonal space in neuroscience, thus qualifies peripersonal space as a 'second skin', a second frontier on which to draw the boundary between the self and the world.

Impact prediction enhances sensory processing of the anticipated event (Blini et al., 2021; Clery and Ben Hamed, 2021). It is useful, however, only if one can prepare one's reactions to it. Ultimately, the multisensory readiness that characterizes peripersonal perception can be explained by the need for motor readiness. To anticipate the snake's potential attack is to be able to react more quickly to it. Peripersonal space is a space in which perceptual content can directly translate into actions, including protective ones (Brozzoli et al., 2012; Bufacchi and Iannetti, 2018; Rizzolatti et al., 1997). When the threat is far away, there are still many possible outcomes and there is still time to ponder what is the best option. By contrast, with spatial proximity comes temporal proximity, which gives rise to specific constraints on the relationship between perception and action. In brief, it is because one has the disposition to act on one's immediate environment that one needs to perceive it in a specific way. This is not to say that peripersonal content represents these dispositions; it is only a claim about the conditions under which a visual experience will have peripersonal content. This account of peripersonal space calls to mind Evans's (1982) dispositional account but restricted to the immediate surroundings of the body. Still, there is an interesting difference between the two. Imagine a creature normally endowed with self-movements but that can no longer move. According to Evans, it suffices for this creature that at one point it had the capacity to move for it to see the world egocentrically. The same is not true for peripersonal space. It has been shown that after only ten hours of immobilization of the right arm, participants show a contraction of the peripersonal space surrounding their arm (Bassolino et al., 2015). Unlike egocentric content, peripersonal content depends on one's *here-and -now* bodily competences.

In virtue of its properties, it has been suggested that peripersonal space defines the space of the self (Serino, 2019). For instance, it has been shown that the RHI works only if the rubber hand is located within peripersonal space. The illusion does not slowly decrease in a linear fashion with the separation increasing between the real hand and the rubber hand. Instead, there is a sudden reduction in the illusion when the rubber hand is positioned beyond the boundaries of peripersonal space (Lloyd, 2007). Within a probabilistic account, one may then say that peripersonal space is the space in which the location of the self is highly likely to be. This, however, does not entail that peripersonal content itself is first-personal, nor does it require the subject to have self-representations. All the mechanisms that characterize peripersonal perception can be described independently of any reference to the first-person. Rather than the space of the self, it may be more accurate to propose that peripersonal space is the space of 'here'. Being here then means being in the small region of space in which one expects the world and the body to collide. This sense of here-ness is relatively primitive, devoid of first-personal content, anchored on bodily location, and based on direct connections between perception and action (Vignemont, 2021). It expresses that what is seen close by is present, not only in the sense that it is spatially connected to one's body but also in the sense that it can act on it, and possibly even hurt it.

4.4 When I Am No Longer There

When one sees the snake next to one's foot, one normally feels that one shares the same space as the snake, but can one lose this sense of being part of a shared space? Though it is hard to conceive what it is like to be deprived of it, it can happen, as illustrated by the psychiatric syndrome of derealization. Derealization is frequently encountered in patients suffering from depersonalization. It includes at least three aspects: (i) a sense of unreality, (ii) a sense of unfamiliarity, and (iii) a sense of disconnection. Patients, for instance, claim: 'It felt as if I was carried extremely far away from this world, and really far' (Dugas and Moutier, 1910, p. 22, my translation); 'I felt as if I was almost entirely separated from the world and as if there was some barrier between me and it' (Dugas and Moutier, 1910, p. 24); 'I feel detached and isolated from the world and the people in it. I feel like I am in a box of very thick glass which stops me from feeling any atmosphere. At times it is like looking at a picture. It has no real depth' (Sierra, 2009, p. 51).

Two main hypotheses compete to account for derealization, in terms respectively of self-awareness and of bodily awareness. Let us start with the first-personal account. Billon (2022) explains all symptoms in depersonalization by a general loss of the sense of mineness. On his view, patients are unable to relate what happens in their mind, body, and world to themselves. As a consequence, they feel detached from their own mental states, from their body, and from their environment, as if they were external observers. A patient, for instance, reported: 'It is not me who feels. I am not interested in what I appear to be feeling, it is somebody else who feels mechanically' (Janet, 1908, p. 515). According to Billon, the loss of mineness explains the sense of body disownership in depersonalized patients, but it may also account for derealization. If patients do not experience their visual and auditory experiences to be their own, then whatever is represented by these experiences has no direct relevance for them. The underlying assumption is that the visual experience of a tree can inform a subject of the presence of the tree in front of him/her only if he/she takes it to be *his/her own* visual experience. In the absence of self-attribution, he/she cannot relate what is seen with his/her location in space. However, one may wonder whether one needs to explain derealization in first-personal terms. There can be a more cognitively modest explanation that tracks the origin of derealization in the disruption of bodily awareness. Patients with depersonalization indeed frequently describe feeling that their body has disappeared: 'I do not feel I have a body. When I look down I see my legs and my body but it feels as if they were not there . . . it feels as if I have no body; I am not there' (Sierra, 2009, p. 28). We have seen that peripersonal space is defined by its proximity with the body. If one mentally loses one's body, then peripersonal space loses its anchor. No sensory or motor deficits have been discovered so far in derealization, but since peripersonal space has not yet been directly tested in patients, it remains an open empirical question whether it could be impaired in this syndrome. We may thus suggest that the impairment of bodily awareness disrupts peripersonal awareness. But can this deficit suffice to explain derealization? The sense of unreality indeed affects the entire environment, and not only what is close to the patients. One may then propose that if one can no longer represent objects as 'here', one can no longer represent them as 'there'. Roughly speaking, by losing peripersonal awareness, one loses one's bridge to the larger world. The perceptual environment then remains simply 'outside'. If this hypothesis is correct, then bodily awareness plays a role – though indirect – for egocentric space in general: bodily space anchors peripersonal space, which in turn anchors the rest of egocentric space.

To conclude, we have shown that bodily awareness anchors us in a larger space full of objects around which we navigate but also from which we must defend ourselves. We are then aware of our immediate surroundings as being real, with the power to be beneficial or detrimental to our body and thus to us. This is true at the level of peripersonal space, but one may propose that it can also be generalized to egocentric space and that bodily awareness contributes to the sense of being present in the world by presenting the locus in which perception meets action.

Outstanding Questions

Throughout this Element, I have uncovered several ways in which the awareness of one's body is like the awareness of no other object, but I have also left a number of issues open. As concluding remarks, I would like to highlight some outstanding questions and show how much more remains to be explored.

First, though most accounts of bodily awareness focus on its multisensory sources, one may wonder about the impact of *cognitive* factors. Are bodily experiences cognitively penetrable? The notions of expectation and prediction have recently been in the limelight, especially in the interpretation of bodily illusions, but their cognitive status remains uncertain. Should we interpret them in doxastic, imaginative, or sensory terms? And what role do they play for the way we experience our body?

A second question concerns the distinction between instrumental and protective agency. I hinted at some differences, but one needs to further investigate to what extent and in what manner they obey different principles. In particular, little is still known about protective agency, and it is unclear how self-centred it is and whether it necessarily bears the mark of the first-person. Furthermore, more interest should be dedicated to bodily awareness in disorders in which one no longer seems to protect one's body, including self-harm behaviours, suicidal tendencies, and depression. Conversely, one should analyse protective responses in patients with bodily disorders, such as personal neglect, anorexia nervosa, and ideomotor apraxia.

The third question specifically targets peripersonal space and its function. I described how the perception of close space presents unique features compared to the perception of far space and briefly alluded to the possibility that peripersonal space could serve as a bridge between the subject and the world. Most literature discusses the contribution of peripersonal space to self-awareness, which is already question-begging, but it remains to be shown how it may also contribute to the awareness of the larger world that awaits us beyond peripersonal space.

A final path will lead us to explore not only the spatial dimension but also the temporal dimension. I argued that bodily awareness anchors our sense of being 'here', but could it also contribute to our sense of being 'now'? Furthermore, what awareness of our body do we keep through time? Unlike perceptual experiences of the world that can remain vivid and detailed in memory, it seems difficult to remember what our body felt like before. Is the inside mode of bodily awareness stuck in the present?

These are only a few examples of the many lines of enquiry still to be explored in the new philosophy of the body.

References

Adams, K. L., Edwards, A., Peart, C., et al. (2022). The association between anxiety and cardiac interoceptive accuracy: A systematic review and meta-analysis. *Neuroscience and Biobehavioral Reviews*, 140, 104754.

Akins, K. (1996). Of sensory systems and the 'aboutness' of mental states. *Journal of Philosophy*, 93(7), 337–72.

Allen, C. (2004). Animal pain. *Noûs*, 38(4), 617–43.

Alsmith, A. J. T. (2015). Mental activity and the sense of ownership. *Review of Philosophy and Psychology*, 6(4), 881–96.

Alsmith, A. J. T. (2017). Perspectival structure and agentive self-location.In F. de Vignemont and A. Alsmith (eds.), *The Subject's Matter: Self-Consciousness and the Body*. Cambridge, MA: MIT Press, pp. 263–88.

Alsmith, A. J. T. (2021). The structure of egocentric space. In F. de Vignemont, A. Serino, H. Y. Wong, and A. Farnè (eds.), *The World at Our Fingertips: A Multidisciplinary Exploration of Peripersonal Space*. Oxford: Oxford University Press, pp. 231–50.

Anema, H. A., van Zandvoort, M. J., de Haan, E. H., et al. (2009). A double dissociation between somatosensory processing for perception and action. *Neuropsychologia*, 47(6), 1615–20.

Anscombe, G. E. M. (1957). *Intention* (2nd ed.). Oxford: Blackwell.

Anscombe, G. E. M. (1962). On sensations of position. *Analysis*, 22(3), 55–8.

Armstrong, D. (1962). *Bodily Sensations*. London: Routledge & Kegan Paul.

Ataria, Y., Tanaka, S., and Gallagher, S. (eds.). (2021). *Body Schema and Body Image: New Directions*. Oxford: Oxford University Press.

Aydede, M. (ed.). (2005). *Pain: New Essays on Its Nature and the Methodology of Its Study*. Cambridge, MA: MIT Press.

Baier, B., and Karnath, H. O. (2008). Tight link between our sense of limb ownership and self-awareness of actions. *Stroke*, 39(2), 486–8.

Bain, D. (2011). The imperative view of pain. *Journal of Consciousness Studies*, 18(9–10), 164–85.

Bain, D. (2013). What makes pains unpleasant?,*Philosophical Studies*, 166(S1), 69–89.

Bain, D. (2014). Pains that don't hurt. *Australasian Journal of Philosophy*, 92(2), 1–16.

Bain, D. (2019). Why take painkillers?, *Nous*, 53(2), 462–90.

Barbot, A., and Carrasco, M. (2018). Emotion and anxiety potentiate the way attention alters visual appearance. *Scientific Reports*, 8(1), 1–10.

Barlassina, L., and Hayward, M. K. (2019a). More of me! Less of me! Reflexive imperativism about affective phenomenal character. *Mind*, 128(512), 1013–44.

Barlassina, L., and Hayward, M. K. (2019b). Loopy regulations. *Philosophical Topics*, 47(2), 233–61.

Bassolino, M., Finisguerra, A., Canzoneri, E., Serino, A., and Pozzo, T. (2015). Dissociating effect of upper limb non-use and overuse on space and body representations. *Neuropsychologia*, 70, 385–92.

Benedetti, F., Pollo, A., Lopiano, L., et al. (2003). Conscious expectation and unconscious conditioning in analgesic, motor, and hormonal placebo/nocebo responses. *Journal of Neuroscience*, 23(10), 4315–23.

Bergqvist, A., and Cowan, R. (eds.). (2018).*Evaluative Perception*. Oxford: Oxford University Press.

Bermúdez, J. L. (1998). *The Paradox of Self-Consciousness*. Cambridge, MA: MIT Press.

Bermúdez, J. L. (2011). Bodily awareness and self-consciousness. In S. Gallagher (ed.), *The Oxford Handbook of the Self*. Oxford: Oxford University Press, pp. 157–79.

Bermúdez, J. L. (2015). Bodily ownership, bodily awareness, and knowledge without observation. *Analysis*, 75(1), 37–45.

Bermúdez, J. L. (2017). Ownership and the space of the body. In F. de Vignemont and A. J. T. Alsmith (eds.), *The Subject's Matter: Self-Consciousness and the Body*. Cambridge, MA: MIT Press, pp. 117–44.

Billon, A. (2017). Mineness first: Three challenges to the recent theories of the sense of bodily ownership. In F. de Vignemont and A. J. T. Alsmith (eds.), *The Subject's Matter: Self-Consciousness and the Body*. Cambridge, MA: MIT Press, pp. 189–216.

Billon, A. (2022). Depersonalization and the sense of bodily ownership. In A. J. T. Alsmith and M. Longo (eds.), *The Routledge Handbook of Bodily Awareness*. London: Routledge, pp. 366–79.

Billon, A. (2023). What is it like to lack mineness? In M. García-Carpintero and M. Guillot (eds.), *Self-Experience: Essays on Inner Awareness*. Oxford: Oxford University Press, pp. 304–42.

Blini, E., Farnè, A., Brozzoli, C., and Hadj-Bouziane, F. (2021). Close is better: Visual perception in peripersonal space. In F. de Vignemont, A. Serino., H. Y. Wong, and A. Farnè (eds.), *The World at Our Fingertips: A Multidisciplinary Exploration of Peripersonal Space*. Oxford: Oxford University Press, pp. 47–60.

Blanke, O., & Arzy, S. (2005). The out-of-body experience: disturbed self-processing at the temporo-parietal junction. The Neuroscientist, 11(1), 16–24.

Block, N. (1996). Mental paint and mental latex. *Philosophical Issues*, 7, 19–49.

Botvinick, M., and Cohen, J. (1998). Rubber hands 'feel' touch that eyes see. *Nature*, 391, 756.

Bouillaud, J.-B. (1825). *Traité clinique et physiologique de l'encéphalite, ou inflammation du cerveau, et de ses suites*. Paris: Chez J.-B. Bailliere.

Bradley, A. (2021). The feeling of bodily ownership. *Philosophy and Phenomenological Research*, 102(2), 359–79.

Brener, J., and Ring, C. (2016). Towards a psychophysics of interoceptive processes: The measurement of heartbeat detection. *Philosophical Transactions of the Royal Society B: Biological Sciences*, 371(1708), 20160015.

Brewer, B. (1992). Self-location and agency. *Mind*, 101(401), 17–34.

Brewer, B. (1995). Bodily awareness and the self. In J. L. Bermúdez, T. Marcel, and N. Eilan (eds.), *The Body and the Self*. Cambridge, MA: MIT Press.

Briscoe, R. E. (2008). Vision, action, and make-perceive. *Mind and Language*, 23(4), 457–97.

Briscoe, R. E. (2009). Egocentric spatial representation in action and perception. *Philosophy and Phenomenological Research*, 79(2), 423–60.

Briscoe, R. (2014). Spatial content and motoric significance. *AVANT*, 5(2), 199–217.

Brozzoli, C., Gentile, G., and Ehrsson, H. H. (2012). That's near my hand! Parietal and premotor coding of hand-centered space contributes to localization and self-attribution of the hand. *Journal of Neuroscience*, 32(42), 14573–82.

Bufacchi, R. J., and Iannetti, G. D. (2018). An action field theory of peripersonal space. *Trends in Cognitive Sciences*, 22(12), 1076–90.

Campbell, J. (2002). *Reference and Consciousness*. Oxford: Clarendon Press.

Cappelen, H., and Dever, J. (2013).*The Inessential Indexical: On the Philosophical Insignificance of Perspective and the First Person*. Oxford: Oxford University Press.

Cardinali, L., Frassinetti, F., Brozzoli, C., et al. (2009). Tool-use induces morphological updating of the body schema. *Current Biology*, 19(12), R478–R479.

Cardinali, L., Zanini, A., Yanofsky, R., et al. (2021). The toolish hand illusion: Embodiment of a tool based on similarity with the hand. *Scientific Reports*, 11(1), 1–9.

Carruthers, P. (2018). Valence and value. *Philosophy and Phenomenological Research*, 97(3), 658–80.

Cassam, Q. (1997). *Self and World*. Oxford: Clarendon Press.

Casser, L., and Clarke, S. (2022). Is pain modular? *Mind and Language*, 38(3), 826–46.

Ceunen, E., Vlaeyen, J. W. S., and Van Diest, I. (2016). On the origin of interoception,*Frontiers in Psychology*, 7.

Chadha, M. (2018). No-self and the phenomenology of ownership.*Australasian Journal of Philosophy*, 96(1), 14–27.

Chamberlain, C. (2022). Not a sailor in his ship: Descartes on bodily awareness. In A. J. T. Alsmith and M. Longo (eds.), *The Routledge Handbook of Bodily Awareness*. London: Routledge, pp. 83–94.

Clark, A. (1997). *Being There: Putting Brain, Body and World Together Again.* Cambridge, MA: MIT Press.

Cléry, J., and Ben Hamed, S (2021). Functional networks for peripersonal space coding and prediction of impact to the body. In F. de Vignemont, A. Serino., H. Y. Wong, and A. Farnè (eds.), *The World at Our Fingertips: A Multidisciplinary Exploration of Peripersonal Space*. Oxford: Oxford University Press, pp. 61–80.

Cogliano, R., Crisci, C., Conson, M., Grossi, D., and Trojano, L. (2012). Chronic somatoparaphrenia: A follow-up study on two clinical cases. *Cortex*, 48(6), 758–67.

Corns, J. (2020). *The Complex Reality of Pain*. London: Routledge.

Craig, A. D. (2010). The sentient self. *Brain Structure and Function*, 214(5–6), 563–77.

Cutter, B., and Tye, M. (2011). Tracking representationalism and the painfulness of pain. *Philosophical Issues*, 21, 90–109.

Damasio, A. R. (1999). *The Feeling of What Happens*. London: William Heinemann.

Danziger, N., and Willer, J. C. (2009). L'insensibilité congénitale à la douleur. *Revue Neurologique*, 165(2), 129–36.

Delevoye-Turrell, Y., Bartolo, A., and Coello, Y. (2010). Motor representation and the perception of space. In N. Gangopadhyay (ed.), *Perception, Action and Consciousness*. Oxford: Oxford University Press, pp. 217–42.

Deonna, J., and Teroni, F. (2012). *The Emotions: A Philosophical Introduction*. London: Routledge.

Descartes, R. (1641/1979). *Les méditations métaphysiques*. Paris: Garnier Flammarion.

Descartes, R. (1643/2018). *Correspondance avec Élisabeth et autres lettres*. Paris: Garnier Flammarion.

Dijkerman, H. C., and de Haan, E. H. (2007). Somatosensory processes subserving perception and action. *The Behavioral and Brain Sciences*, 30(2), 189–201.

Dokic, J. (2003). The sense of ownership: An analogy between sensation and action. In J. Roessler and N. Eilan (eds.), *Agency and Self-Awareness: Issues in Philosophy and Psychology*. Oxford: Oxford University Press, pp. 321–44.

Dokic, J., and Martin, J. R. (2015). 'Looks the same but feels different': A metacognitive approach to cognitive penetrability. In A. Raftopoulos and Zeimbekis, J. (eds), *Cognitive Effects on Perception: New Philosophical Perspectives*. Oxford: Oxford University Press, pp. 240–67.

Dokic, J., and Martin, J. R. (2017). Felt reality and the opacity of perception. *Topoi*, 36(2), 299–309.

Dugas, L., and Moutier, F. (1910). Dépersonnalisation et émotion. *Revue Philosophique de la France et de l'Étranger*, 70, 441–60.

Ehrsson, H. H., Fotopoulou, A., Radziun, D., Longo, M., and Tsakiris, M. (2022). No specific relationship between hypnotic suggestibility and the rubber hand illusion: A commentary with new and verification analyses. *Nature Communication*, 13, 564.

Ehrsson, H. H., Wiech, K., Weiskopf, N., Dolan, R. J., and Passingham, R. E. (2007). Threatening a rubber hand that you feel is yours elicits a cortical anxiety response. *Proceedings of the National Academy of Sciences of the United States of America*, 104(23), 9828–33.

Eilan, N., McCarthy, R., and Brewer, B. (1993). General introduction. In N. Eilan, R. McCarthy, and B. Brewer (eds.), *Spatial Representation: Problems in Philosophy and Psychology*, New York: Oxford University Press, pp. 1–22.

Evans, G. (1982). *The Varieties of Reference*. Oxford: Oxford University Press.

Evans, G. (1985). Molyneux's question. In *The Collected Papers of Gareth Evans*. Oxford: Oxford University Press, pp. 364–99.

Ferentzi, E., Bogdany, T., Szabolcs, Z., et al. (2018). Multichannel investigation of interoception: Sensitivity is not a generalizable feature. *Frontiers in Human Neuroscience*, 12, 223.

Fourneret, P., and Jeannerod, M. (1998). Limited conscious monitoring of motor performance in normal subjects. *Neuropsychologia*, 36(11), 1133–40.

Frances, A., and Gale, L. (1975). The proprioceptive body image in self-object differentiation: A case of congenital indifference to pain and head-banging. *The Psychoanalytic Quarterly*, 44(1), 107–26.

Fulkerson, M. (2020). Emotional perception. *Australasian Journal of Philosophy*, 98(1), 16–30.

Fulkerson, M. (2023). How thirst compels: An aggregation model of sensory motivation. *Mind and Language*, 38(1), 141–55.

Gallagher, S. (2003). Bodily self-awareness and object perception. *Theoria et Historia Scientiarum*, 7(1), 53–68.

Gallagher, S. (2005). *How the Body Shapes the Mind*. New York: Oxford University Press.

Gallagher, S. (2022). Bodily self-awareness and body-schematic processes. In A. J. T. Alsmith and M. Longo (eds.), *The Routledge Handbook of Bodily Awareness*. London: Routledge.

Gallagher, S., and Cole, J. (1995). Body schema and body image in a deafferented subject. *Journal of Mind and Behaviour*, 16(4), 369–90.

Garfinkel, S. N., Manassei, M. F., Hamilton-Fletcher, G., et al. (2016). Interoceptive dimensions across cardiac and respiratory axes. *Philosophical Transactions of the Royal Society B: Biological Sciences*, 371(1708),

Garfinkel, S. N., Seth, A. K., Barrett, A. B., Suzuki, K., and Critchley, H. D. (2015). Knowing your own heart: Distinguishing interoceptive accuracy from interoceptive awareness. *Biological Psychology*, 104, 65–74.

Gligorov, N. (2017). Don't worry, this will only hurt a bit: The role of expectation and attention in pain intensity. *The Monist*, 100(4), 501–13.

González-Franco, M., Peck, T. C., Rodríguez-Fornells, A., and Slater, M. (2013). A threat to a virtual hand elicits motor cortex activation. *Experimental Brain Research*, 232(3), 875–87.

Grahek, N. (2001). *Feeling Pain and Being in Pain*. Cambridge, MA: MIT Press.

Graziano, M. (2018). *The Spaces between Us: A Story of Neuroscience, Evolution, and Human Nature*. New York: Oxford University Press.

Grice, H. P. (1962). Some remarks about the senses. In R. J. Butler (ed.), *Analytical Philosophy: First Series*. Oxford: Oxford University Press, pp. 133–53.

Grush, R. (2004). The emulation theory of representation: Motor control, imagery, and perception. *Behavioral and Brain Sciences*, 27, 377–96.

Gurwitsch, A. (1985). *Marginal Consciousness*. Athens: Ohio University Press.

Hediger, H. (1955). *Studies of the Psychology and Behavior of Captive Animals in Zoos and Circuses*. London: Butterworth and Co.

Hall, E. (1966). *The Hidden Dimension*. Albany, NY: Anchor Books.

Hall, R. J. (2008). If it itches, scratch!*Australasian Journal of Philosophy*, 86(4), 525–35.

Hurley, S. (1998). *Consciousness in Action*. Cambridge, MA: Harvard University Press.

Husserl, E. (1952/1989). *Ideas Pertaining to a Pure Phenomenology and to a Phenomenological Philosophy: Second Book*, trans. R. Rojcewicz and A. Schuwer. Dordrecht: Kluwer Academic Publishers.

Jacobson, H. (2013). Killing the messenger: Representationalism and the painfulness of pain. *The Philosophical Quarterly*, 63(252), 509–19.

Jacobson, H. (2021). The role of valence in perception: An ARTistic treatment. *Philosophical Review*, 130(4), 481–531.

Janet, P. (1908). Le sentiment de dépersonnalisation. *Journal de psychologie normale et pathologique*, 5, 514–16.

Kammers, M. P. M., F. de Vignemont, L. Verhagen, and H. C. Dijkerman (2009). The rubber hand illusion in action.*Neuropsychologia*, 47(1), 204–11.

Kaplan, D. (1989). Demonstratives. In J. Almog, J. Perry, and H. Wettstein (eds.), *Themes from Kaplan*. Oxford: Oxford University Press, pp. 481–563.

Klein, C. (2015a). *What the Body Commands: The Imperative Theory of Pain*. Cambridge, MA: MIT Press.

Klein, C. (2015b). What pain asymbolia really shows. *Mind*, 124(494), 493–516.

Klein, C., and Martínez, M. (2018). Imperativism and pain intensity. In J. Corns (ed.), *The Routledge Handbook of Philosophy of Pain*. London: Routledge, pp. 13–26.

Lang, P. J., and Bradley, M. M. (2013). Appetitive and defensive motivation: Goal-directed or goal-determined?. *Emotion Review*, 5(3), 230–4.

Leder, D. (2018). Inside insights: A phenomenology of interoception. In M. Tsakiris and H. de Preester (eds.), *The Interoceptive Mind: From Homeostasis to Awareness*. Oxford: Oxford University Press, 307–22.

LeDoux, J., and Daw, N. D. (2018). Surviving threats: Neural circuit and computational implications of a new taxonomy of defensive behaviour. *Nature Reviews Neuroscience*, 19(5), 269–82.

Lenggenhager, B. and Ho, J. T. (2022). Out-of-body experiences. In A. J. T. Alsmith and M. Longo (eds.), *The Routledge Handbook of Bodily Awareness*. London: Routledge, pp. 411–23.

Lenggenhager, B., Tadi, T., Metzinger, T., and Blanke, O. (2007). Video ergo sum: Manipulating bodily self-consciousness. *Science*, 317(5841), 109.6–109.9.

Lewis, D. (1980). Mad pain and Martian pain. *Readings in the Philosophy of Psychology*, 1, 216–22.

Lloyd, D. M. (2007). Spatial limits on referred touch to an alien limb may reflect boundaries of visuo-tactile peripersonal space surrounding the hand. *Brain and Cognition*, 64(1), 104–9.

Longo, M. R., Schüür, F., Kammers, M. P., Tsakiris, M., and Haggard, P. (2008). What is embodiment? A psychometric approach. *Cognition*, 107(3), 978–98.

Lush, P. (2020). Demand characteristics confound the rubber hand illusion. *Collabra: Psychology*, 6(1), 22.

Lush, P., Botan, V., Scott, R. B., et al. (2020). Trait phenomenological control predicts experience of mirror synaesthesia and the rubber hand illusion. *Nature Communications*, 11(1), 1–10.

McDowell, J. (2011). Anscombe on bodily self-knowledge. In A. Ford, J. Hornsby, and F. Stoutland (eds.), *Essays on Anscombe's 'Intention'*. Cambridge, MA: MIT Press, pp. 128–46.

Ma, K., and Hommel, B. (2015). The role of agency for perceived ownership in the virtual hand illusion. *Consciousness and Cognition*, 36, 277–88.

Malebranche, N. (1674/1980). *The Search after Truth*, trans. T. M. Lennon. Columbus: Ohio State University Press.

Mandrigin, A. (2021). The where of bodily awareness. *Synthese*, 198(3), 1887–903.

Maratos, F. A., and Pessoa, L. (2019). What drives prioritized visual processing? A motivational relevance account. *Progress in Brain Research*, 247, 111–48.

Maravita, A. (2008). Spatial disorders. In S. F. Cappa, J. Abutalebi, J. F. Demonet, P. C. Fletcher, and P. Garrard (eds.), *Cognitive Neurology: A Clinical Textbook*. New York: Oxford University Press, pp. 89–118.

Martin, M. G. F. (1992). Sight and touch. In T. Crane (ed.), *The Content of Experience*. Cambridge: Cambridge University Press, pp. 199–201.

Martin, M. G. F. (1995). Bodily awareness: A sense of ownership. In J. L. Bermúdez, T. Marcel, and N. Eilan (eds.), *The Body and the Self*. Cambridge, MA: MIT Press.

Martínez, M. (2011). Imperative content and the painfulness of pain. *Phenomenology and the Cognitive Sciences*, 10(1), 67–90.

Martínez, M. (2015). Disgusting smells and imperativism, *Journal of Consciousness Studies*, 22(5–6), 191–200.

Martínez, M. (2022). Imperative transparency. *Mind*, 131(522), 585–601.

Medina, J. (2022). Distinguishing body representations. In A. J. T. Alsmith and M. Longo (eds.), *The Routledge Handbook of Bodily Awareness*. London: Routledge, pp. 150–60.

Melzack, R. (1990). Phantom limbs and the concept of a neuromatrix. *Trends in Neuroscience*, 13(3), 88–92.

Melzack, R., and Wall, P. D. (1983). *The Challenge of Pain*. New York: Basic Books

Merleau-Ponty, M. (1945). *Phénoménologie de la perception*. Paris: Gallimard.

Metzinger, T. (2005). Out-of-body experiences as the origin of the concept of a 'soul'. *Mind and Matter*, 3(1), 57–84.

Miall, R. C., Afanasyeva, D., Cole, J. D., and Mason, P. (2021). The role of somatosensation in automatic visuo-motor control: A comparison of congenital and acquired sensory loss. *Experimental Brain Research*, 239(7), 2043–61.

Miller, L. E., Montroni, L., Koun, E., et al. (2018). Sensing with tools extends somatosensory processing beyond the body. *Nature*, 561(7722), 239–42.

Millikan, R. G. (1990). The myth of the essential indexical. *Noûs*, 24(5), 723–34.

Millikan, R. G. (1995). Pushmi-pullyu representations. *Philosophical Perspectives*, 9, 185–200.

Milner, A. D., and Goodale, M. A. (2008). Two visual systems re-viewed. *Neuropsychologia*, 46(3), 774–85.

Mitchell, J. (2021). *Emotion As Feeling towards Value*. Oxford: Oxford University Press.

Mitchell, S. W. (1871). Phantom limbs. *Lippincott's Magazine of Popular Literature and Science*, 8, 563–9.

Moore, G. E. (1903). The refutation of idealism.*Mind*, 12(48), 433–53.

Moro, V., Zampini, M., and Aglioti, S. M. (2004). Changes in spatial position of hands modify tactile extinction but not disownership of contralesional hand in two right brain-damaged patients. *Neurocase*, 10(6), 437–43.

Noë, A. (2004). *Action in Perception*. Cambridge, MA: MIT Press.

Noë, A. (2010). Vision without Representation. In N. Gangopadhyay, M. Madary, and F. Spicer (eds.), *Perception, Action and Consciousness*. Oxford: Oxford University Press, pp. 245–56.

O'Callaghan, C. (2019). *A Multisensory Philosophy of Perception*. Oxford: Oxford University Press.

O'Regan, K. (2011). *Why Red Doesn't Sound Like a Bell*. Oxford: Oxford University Press.

O'Shaughnessy, B. (1980). *The Will*, vol. 1. Cambridge: Cambridge University Press.

O'Shaughnessy, B. (1995). Proprioception and the body image. In J. L. Bermúdez, T. Marcel, and N. Eilan (eds.), *The Body and the Self*. Cambridge, MA: MIT Press, pp. 175–203.

Olausson, H., Cole, J., Rylander, K., et al. (2008). Functional role of unmyelinated tactile afferents in human hairy skin: Sympathetic response and perceptual localization. *Experimental Brain Research*, 184(1), 135–40.

Olson, E. (1997). *The Human Animal: Personal Identity without Psychology*. Oxford: Oxford University Press.

Paillard, J. (1999). Body schema and body image: A double dissociation in deafferented patients. In G. N. Gantchev, S. Mori, and J. Massion (eds.), *Motor Control, Today and Tomorrow*. Sofia: Academic Publishing House, pp. 197–214.

Paillard, J., Michel, F., and Stelmach, G. (1983). Localization without content: A tactile analogue of 'blind sight'. *Archives of Neurology*, 40(9), 548–51.

Pastore, R. E. (1987). Categorical perception: Some psychophysical models. In S. Harnad (ed.), *Categorical Perception: The Groundwork of Cognition*. New York: Cambridge University Press, pp. 29–52.

Peacocke, C. (2000). *Being Known*. Oxford: Oxford University Press.

Peacocke, C. (2014). *The Mirror of the World: Subjects, Consciousness, and Self-Consciousness*. Oxford: Oxford University Press.

Peacocke, C. (2016). The nature and role of first- and second-person content. *Analysis*, 76(3), 345–54.

Peacocke, C. (2017). Philosophical reflections on the first person. In F. de Vignemont and A. Alsmith (eds.), *The Subject's Matter: Self-Consciousness and the Body*. Cambridge, MA: MIT Press, pp. 289–310.

Perry, J. (1993). *The Problem of the Essential Indexical: And other Essays*. Oxford: Oxford University Press.

Pitron, V., Alsmith, A., and de Vignemont, F. (2018). How do the body schema and the body image interact? *Consciousness and Cognition*, 65, 352–8.

Pouget, A., Deneve, S., and Duhamel, J.-R. (2002). A computational perspective on the neural basis of multisensory spatial representations. *Nature Reviews Neuroscience*, 3, 741–7.

Pourtois, G., Schettino, A., and Vuilleumier, P. (2013). Brain mechanisms for emotional influences on perception and attention: What is magic and what is not. *Biological Psychology*, 92(3), 492–512.

Price, D. D. (2000). Psychological and neural mechanisms of the affective dimension of pain. *Science*, 288(5472), 1769–72.

Richardson, L. (2017). Sight and the body. In F. de Vignemont and A. Alsmith (eds.), *The Subject's Matter: Self-Consciousness and the Body*. Cambridge, MA: MIT Press, pp. 239–62.

Rizzolatti, G., Fadiga, L., Fogassi, L., and Gallese, V. (1997). The space around us. *Science*, 277(5323), 190–1.

Rizzolatti, G., Scandolara, C., Matelli, M., and Gentilucci, M. (1981). Afferent properties of periarcuate neurons in macaque monkeys. II: Visual responses. *Behavioural Brain Research*, 2(2), 147–63.

Röder, B., Kusmierek, A., Spence, C., and Schicke, T. (2007). Developmental vision determines the reference frame for the multisensory control of action. *Proceedings of the National Academy of Sciences*, 104(11), 4753–8.

Romano, D., Gandola, M., Bottini, G., and Maravita, A. (2014). Arousal responses to noxious stimuli in somatoparaphrenia and anosognosia: Clues to body awareness. *Brain*, 137(Pt 4): 1213–23.

Romano, D., and Maravita, A. (2019). The dynamic nature of the sense of ownership after brain injury: Clues from asomatognosia and somatoparaphrenia, *Neuropsychologia*, 132, 107–19.

Rossetti, Y., Rode, G., and Boisson, D. (1995). Implicit processing of somaesthetic information: A dissociation between where and how? *Neuroreport*, 6(3), 506–10.

Schellenberg, S. (2007). Action and self-location in perception. *Mind*, 116(463), 603–32.

Schwenkler, J. (2014). Vision, self-location, and the phenomenology of the 'point of view'. *Noûs*, 48(1), 137–55.

Serino A. (2019). Peripersonal space (PPS) as a multisensory interface between the individual and the environment, defining the space of the self. *Neuroscience & Biobehavioral Reviews*, 99, 138–59.

Serrahima, C. (2023). The bounded body: On the sense of bodily ownership and the experience of space. In M. Garcia-Carpintero and M. Guillot (eds.), *Self-Experience: Essays on Inner Awareness*. Oxford: Oxford University Press, pp. 250–68.

Seth, A. (2013). Interoceptive inference, emotion, and the embodied self. *Trends in Cognitive Science*, 17(11), 565–73.

Shoemaker, S. (1968). Self-reference and self-awareness. *Journal of Philosophy*, 65(19), 555–67.

Shoemaker, S. (1976). Embodiment and behavior. In A. O. Rorty (ed.), *The Identity of Persons*. Berkeley: University of California Press, pp. 109–37.

Shoemaker, S. (1999). Self, body, and coincidence. *Proceedings of the Aristotelian Society* (supplementary Volume), 73, 287–306.

Schwoebel, J. and Coslett, H. B. (2005). Evidence for multiple, distinct representations of the human body.*Journal of Cognitive Neuroscience*, 17(4), 543–53.

Shepherd, J. (2015). Conscious control over action. *Mind and Language*, 30(3), 320–44.

Sherrington, C. S. (1906). *The Integrative Action of the Nervous System*. New Haven, CT: Yale University Press.

Shevlin, H., and Friesen, P. (2021). Pain, placebo, and cognitive penetration. *Mind and Language*, 36(5), 771–91.

Siegel, S. (2010). *The Contents of Visual Experience*. New York: Oxford University Press.

Sierra, M. (2009). *Depersonalization: A New Look at a Neglected Syndrome*. Cambridge: Cambridge University Press.

Simmons, A. (2008). Guarding the body: A Cartesian phenomenology of perception. In P. Hoffman, D. Owen, and G. Yaffe (eds.), *Contemporary Perspectives on Early Modern Philosophy: Essays in Honor of Vere Chappell*. Peterborough, ON: Broadview Press, pp. 81–113.

Skarbez, R., Neyret, S., Brooks, F. P., Slater, M., and Whitton, M. C. (2017). A psychophysical experiment regarding components of the plausibility illusion. *IEEE Transactions on Visualization and Computer Graphics*, 23(4), 1369–78.

Slater, M., Spanlang, B., and Corominas, D. (2010). Simulating virtual environments within virtual environments as the basis for a psychophysics of presence. *ACM Transactions on Graphics (TOG)*, 29(4), 1–9.

Slater, M., Spanlang, B., Sanchez-Vives, M. V., and Blanke, O. (2010). First person experience of body transfer in virtual reality. *PloS One*, 5(5), e10564.

Smith, A. D. (2002). *The Problem of Perception*. Cambridge, MA: Harvard University Press.

Snowdon, P. F. (1991). Personal identity and brain transplants. *Royal Institute of Philosophy Supplements*, 29, 109–26.

Spence, C., Pavani, F., and Driver, J. (2004). Spatial constraints on visual-tactile cross-modal distractor congruency effects. *Cognitive, Affective, and Behavioral Neuroscience*, 4(2), 148–69.

Suksasilp, C., and Garfinkel, S. N. (2022). Towards a comprehensive assessment of interoception in a multi-dimensional framework. *Biological Psychology*, 168, 108262.

Tammero, L. F., and Dickinson, M. H. (2002). Collision-avoidance and landing responses are mediated by separate pathways in the fruit fly *Drosophila Melanogaster*. *Journal of Experimental Biology*, 205(18), 2785–98.

Tappolet, C. (2016). *Emotions, Values and Agency*. Oxford: Oxford University Press.

Taylor, C. (1964). *The Explanation of Behaviour*. London: Routledge.

Tsakiris, M. (2017). The material me. In F. de Vignemont and A. Alsmith (eds.), *The Subject's Matter: Self-Consciousness and the Body*. Cambridge, MA: MIT Press, pp. 335–62.

Tsakiris, M. and de Preester, H. (eds.) (2018). *The Interoceptive Mind: From Homeostasis to Awareness*. Oxford: Oxford University Press.

de Vignemont, F. (2007). Habeas corpus: The sense of ownership of one's own body. *Mind and Language*, 22(4), 427–49.

de Vignemont, F. (2010). Body schema and body image: Pros and cons. *Neuropsychologia*, 48(3), 669–80.

de Vignemont, F. (2011). A mosquito bite against the enactive view to bodily experiences. *Journal of Philosophy*, 108(4), 188–204.

de Vignemont, F. (2015). Pain and bodily care: Whose body matters? *Australasian Journal of Philosophy*, 93(3), 542–60.

de Vignemont, F. (2018). *Mind the Body*. Oxford: Oxford University Press.

de Vignemont, F. (2020). What phenomenal contrast for bodily ownership? *Journal of the American Philosophy Association*, 6(1), 117–37.

de Vignemont, F. (2021). A minimal sense of here-ness. *Journal of Philosophy*, 118(4), 169–87.

de Vignemont, F. (2023). Fifty shades of affective colouring of perception. *Australasian Journal of Philosophy*, 101(1): 1–15.

de Vignemont, F., Majid, A., Jola, C., and Haggard, P. (2009). Segmenting the body into parts: Evidence from biases in tactile perception. *Quarterly Journal of Experimental Psychology*, 62(3), 500–12.

de Vignemont, F., Serino, A., Wong, H. Y., and Farnè, A. (eds.) (2021). *The World at Our Fingertips: A Multidisciplinary Exploration of Peripersonal Space*. Oxford: Oxford University Press.

Wager, T. D., Rilling, J. K., Smith, E. E., et al. (2004). Placebo-induced changes in FMRI in the anticipation and experience of pain. *Science*, 303(5661), 1162–7.

Welch, R. B., Widawski, M. H., Harrington, J., and Warren, D. H. (1979). An examination of the relationship between visual capture and prism adaptation. *Perception and Psychophysics*, 25(2), 126–32.

Wong, H. Y. (2009). On the necessity of bodily awareness for bodily action. *Psyche*, 15(1).

Wong, H. Y. (2015). On the significance of bodily awareness for action. *Philosophical Quarterly*, 65(261): 790–812.

Wong, H. Y. (2017). On proprioception in action: Multimodality versus deafferentation. *Mind and Language*, 32(3), 259–82.

Wong, H. Y. (2018). Embodied agency. *Philosophy and Phenomenological Research*, 97(3), 584–612.

Wu, W. (2023). Mineness and introspective data. In M. Garcia-Carpintero and M. Guillot (eds.), *Self-Experience: Essays on Inner Awareness*. Oxford: Oxford University Press, pp. 120–41.

Zanini, A., Patané, I., Blini, E., et al. (2021). Peripersonal and reaching space differ: Evidence from their spatial extent and multisensory facilitation pattern. *Psychonomic Bulletin and Review*, 28(6), 1894–905.

Cambridge Elements ≡

Philosophy of Mind

Keith Frankish

The University of Sheffield
Keith Frankish is a philosopher specializing in philosophy of mind, philosophy of psychology, and philosophy of cognitive science. He is the author of *Mind and Supermind* (Cambridge University Press, 2004) and *Consciousness* (2005), and has also edited or coedited several collections of essays, including *The Cambridge Handbook of Cognitive Science* (Cambridge University Press, 2012), *The Cambridge Handbook of Artificial Intelligence* (Cambridge University Press, 2014) (both with William Ramsey), and *Illusionism as a Theory of Consciousness* (2017).

About the Series

This series provides concise, authoritative introductions to contemporary work in philosophy of mind, written by leading researchers and including both established and emerging topics. It provides an entry point to the primary literature and will be the standard resource for researchers, students, and anyone wanting a firm grounding in this fascinating field.

Cambridge Elements ☰

Philosophy of Mind

Elements in the Series

Mindreading and Social Cognition
Jane Suilin Lavelle

Free Will
Derk Pereboom

Philosophy of Neuroscience
William Bechtel and Linus Ta-Lun Huang

The Metaphysics of Mind
Janet Levin

Mental Illness
Tim Thornton

Imagination and Creative Thinking
Amy Kind

Attention and Mental Control
Carolyn Dicey Jennings

Biological Cognition
Bryce Huebner and Jay Schulkin

Embodied and Enactive Approaches to Cognition
Shaun Gallagher

Mental Content
Peter Schulte

Affective Bodily Awareness
Frédérique de Vignemont

A full series listing is available at: www.cambridge.org/EPMI

Printed in the United States
by Baker & Taylor Publisher Services